BERNSTEIN
REMEMBERED

Introduction by Donal Henahan
Preface by Isaac Stern

Edited by Jane Fluegel
Designed by Martin Moskof

...bute to Leonard Bernstein is a little like carving Mount Rushmore. ...s of Bernstein as composer, conductor, pianist, and teacher is a daunting but

...owed the photographers credited on the pages that follow. Their ...iasm, as well as that of their representatives, are deeply appreciated. ...to thank the following archivists, musicologists, researchers, and lenders who ...is book a reality: Boston Symphony Orchestra: Bridget Blagbrough and Steven Ledbetter; Columbia University School of Journalism: Nathalie Paine; Sir Leonard Conner; Curtis Institute of Music: Ann Diebold; Peter Hensel; Ken Heyman Photography: Enid Mastrianni; Peter Kazaras; Kennedy Center for the Performing Arts: Joan Marcus; Beth Kugler; Ann Littlejohn; Magnum Photos; Madeleine Matz; Metropolitan Opera Archives: John Pennino; The Museum of Modern Art: Mary Corliss, Susan Kismaric, Rona Roob, Charles Silver, and Karen Starr; Museum of the City of New York; Junichi Nakajima; New York Philharmonic Archives: Barbara Haws and Chris Willard; New York Public Library, Dance, Music, and Theater Collections; Ruth Orkin Estate: Mary Engel; Ann Phalon; Nicolas Slonimsky; Sony Music: Josephine Mangiaracina and Tina McCarthy; Vienna Philharmonic: The Mses. Stuckhammer and Heindl; Wisconsin Center for Film and Theater Research: Maxine Ducey; Electra Yourke.

Isaac Stern has been a most willing and loving participant in this enterprise, and Stephen Sondheim most generous in contributing his witty birthday song. To Donal Henahan, soon to retire as chief music critic of *The New York Times*, my thanks for his deft overview of Bernstein's long career.

Finally, a special word of thanks to my editors, Sheila Cavanagh and Peter Skutches, and my publisher, Richard Gallen. Jill Gallen has been a special friend throughout. And Harvey Phillips deserves a month in the country for all his help.

J.F.

Conceived by Jill Gallen
Design by Martin Moskof Associates Inc.
Text and captions by Jane Fluegel
Additional text by Hettie Jones, Eric Richards, Harvey E. Phillips and Gary Ginstling

Copyright © 1991 by Carroll & Graf Publishers, Inc.
Introduction copyright © 1990 by The New York Times Company.
Reprinted by permission.

Preface copyright © 1991 by Isaac Stern

Lyrics for "Leonard Bernstein's 70th Birthday Song" copyright © 1988 by Stephen Sondheim.
Reprinted by permission.

Lyrics for "Make Our Garden Grow," from *Candide* copyright
© 1955, 1958, 1974, 1982 by Leonard Bernstein.
Copyright renewed by JALNI Publications/Boosey & Hawkes. Reprinted by permission.

Lyrics for "New York, New York," from *On the Town*, copyright © 1944 by Warner-Chappell.
Reprinted by permission.

All photographs by Steve J. Sherman, copyright © the photographer.

All rights reserved

First Carroll & Graf edition 1991

Carroll & Graf Publishers, Inc.
260 Fifth Avenue
New York, NY 10001

Library of Congress Cataloging-in-Publication Data

Bernstein remembered : a life in pictures / edited by Jane Fluegel :
    introduction by Donal Henahan : preface by Isaac Stern.
    —1st Carroll & Graf ed.
        p.   cm.
    ISBN 0-88184-722-4 : $32.00
    1. Bernstein, Leonard, 1918–   —Portraits.
    2. Musicians—Portraits. I. Fluegel, Jane.
    ML88.B476B47   1991
    780'.92—dc20
    [B]   91-21739
                                                                              CIP
                                                                              MN

Type composition by Trufont Typographers, Inc.
Printed and bound by Berryville Graphics, Berryville, Virginia
Manufactured in the United States of America

Page 1:
Conducting the Israel
Philharmonic at Carnegie
Hall, New York,
September 1986.
Photograph by Steve J. Sherman

Frontispiece:
Conducting the Chicago
Symphony Orchestra, Avery
Fisher Hall, New York,
June 1988.
Photograph by Steve J. Sherman

CONTENTS

Top: Bernstein and Stern in Israel, 1957, at the dedication of the Frederic Mann Auditorium, Tel Aviv, new home of the Israel Philharmonic Orchestra. *Photograph by D. Rubinger, courtesy Isaac Stern. Above left:* With violinist Isaac Stern in Venice, 1954, where Stern was soloist in and Bernstein conducted the world premiere of his Serenade for Solo Violin, Harp, Percussion, and Strings, played by the Israel Philharmonic Orchestra. *Photograph courtesy Isaac Stern. Above right:* Bernstein congratulates Stern at the reopening concert at Carnegie Hall, New York, on December 15, 1986, shortly after renovation of the hall (in which Stern played a leading role) was completed. *Photograph by Steve J. Sherman.*

PREFACE

by Isaac Stern

In his introduction to this book, Donal Henahan has given a clear, detailed, and sympathetic overview of the life and accomplishments of the blazing meteor we knew as Leonard Bernstein. To millions of music lovers, musicians, actors, statesmen, dancers, writers, doormen, and taxi drivers, from Boston to Buenos Aires, from Tokyo to Tel Aviv, from Malibu to Moscow, Lenny was familiar, recognized, and adored.

We first met in New York in 1946, at the home of mutual friends. The following year, in Rochester, New York, we played our first concert together, the beginning of almost four decades of close friendship and musical collaboration.

In these few lines it is impossible to encapsulate the special moments we had, on stage and off—in New York, Los Angeles, and Jerusalem, Venice, Florence, and Rome; sometimes they were in recording rooms and, most happily, at home. To make music with him was always an adventure; nothing was taken for granted. Together we shared the quest for a deeper subtlety, a sharper contrast, a sudden burst of energy, or a sustained quiet, long line. Most of all, it was all so alive; and nothing was ever done casually.

Had he wanted to follow only one discipline more determinedly, he could well have been a great concert pianist. It was astonishing how with almost no steady practice immediately preceding a rehearsal or performance, he would complain about lack of time, stretch his interlocked hands with palms turned out, crack a knuckle or two, and proceed to make some ravishingly beautiful sounds at the piano.

Most of all, I remember long talks about music, people, history, family, and the world around us, the last of these only a few short weeks before he died. These are my most personal memories of Lenny: his incredible mind, insatiable in its lust for knowledge, devouring volumes of poetry, history, biography, and philosophy, reveling in the power and beauty of ideas, driven to share his wonder at these human treasures with all who were around him—most particularly young people.

He had a passion for teaching—on television, in classes, through his writing and conducting, or just having drinks and dinner. Russian novels, French poems, Shakespeare, the Bible, the written history of man's mind, were his roaming fields; the most intricate and arcane of crossword puzzles and word games his delights.

All this was brought to bear on his music-making and his creative vitality. In his last years he found himself ever more involved with the indefinable magic of music. He would exclaim, with a sense of wonder in his voice, how, in going back to perform once again a Brahms symphony—or one by Tchaikovsky or Mahler—he had to take a clean score, unmarked by his analyses of previous years, in order to look at the music with fresh eyes, discovering still greater beauties hidden within those lines and dots on white paper. He found renewed delight in those small spaces between the notes where music truly is made. This constant questioning of past assumptions seems to belie, at least to me, the statement he made some years earlier: "I don't want to spend my life . . . studying and restudying the same fifty pieces of music. It would bore me to death. I want to conduct . . . to play the piano . . . to write symphonic music . . . to keep on trying to be in the full sense of that wonderful word a musician."

He, and we even more, were fortunate that his multi-faceted talents came to full flower just as television began to be the dominant medium of the second half of the twentieth century, while the recording industry, with dizzying technical changes every few years, added additional impulse to the growing, powerful performances of Leonard Bernstein in the concert hall and musical theater, in films, in opera houses and open fields from Mount Scopus in Jerusalem to the Berlin Wall, all brought constantly to the world's attention. He was the most visible and the most recorded performer of his time, unarguably *the* American in music everywhere. He was a determined humanist, believing in the absolute necessity of decency. He was a wonderful, loyal friend.

It is so hard to think that one cannot pick up the phone and hear that warm, gravelly voice smiling a hello.

INTRODUCTION

Donal Henahan

Leonard Bernstein, one of the most prodigally talented and successful musicians in American history, died at his home in New York City on October 14, 1990, just five days after the announcement that he would retire from performing because of health problems. In the months preceding, he had canceled concerts in Japan and the United States, as well as a tour of Europe. He conducted his final performance at Tanglewood, in the Berkshires of Western Massachusetts, on August 19, 1990, when he led the Boston Symphony Orchestra in Britten's Four Sea Interludes and Beethoven's Seventh Symphony.

Long before Bernstein became, at the age of forty, the youngest music director ever engaged by the New York Philharmonic, the drama critic Harold Clurman sized up the flamboyant musician's future: "Lenny is hopelessly fated for success."

It was Leonard Bernstein's fate to be far more than routinely successful, however. His fast-burning energies, his bewildering versatility, and his profuse gifts for both music and theater coalesced to make him a high-profile figure in a dozen fields, among them symphonic music, Broadway musicals, the ballet, film, and television.

Still, his hydra-headed success did not please all his critics. While he was music director of the New York Philharmonic from 1958 to 1969, some friends and critics urged him to quit and compose theater music full time. Many regarded him as the potential savior of the American musical, to which he contributed scores for *On the Town, Wonderful Town, Candide,* and *West Side Story.*

At the same time, others were deploring his continued activity in such fields, contending

that to be a successful leader of a major orchestra he would have to focus on conducting. Still other observers of the Bernstein phenomenon wished he would concentrate on the ballet, for which he had shown an affinity (*Fancy Free, Facsimile*), or on opera and operetta (*Trouble in Tahiti, Candide*). Or on musical education. His television programs on such subjects as conducting, symphonic music, and jazz fascinated millions when he appeared on Omnibus, the cultural series, and later as the star of the Philharmonic's own televised Young People's Concerts.

And still others, a loyal few, counseled Bernstein to throw it all over and compose more serious symphonic scores. His gifts along this line were apparent in such works as his Symphony No. 1 (*Jeremiah*) of 1942, Symphony No. 2 (*The Age of Anxiety*) of 1949, and Symphony No. 3 (*Kaddish*) of 1963. He played the piano well enough to have made a separate career as a virtuoso. He was a gifted poet. He wrote several books, including the popular *Joy of Music* (1959). He was a teacher of rare communicative talent, as television audiences discovered. But Bernstein resolutely resisted pressure to restrict his activities. During his eleven years as the Philharmonic's music director, he grew steadily as an interpreter and as a technician.

A Musical Obsession Became a Boom

Bernstein's performances of Mahler's symphonies were almost universally conceded to be of the highest quality, and his recording of all nine for Columbia Records constituted the first such integral collection. They continue to be regarded as among the most idiomatic Mahler performances available. In fact, Bernstein's obsession with that composer has been credited

Top:
Bernstein conducting the New York Philharmonic in a performance of *Kaddish,* his Symphony No. 3, with his wife, Felicia, as Speaker, April 1964.
Photograph by Don Hunstein, Sony Music

Bottom:
Gustav Mahler, c. 1907.
New York Public Library, Music Division

Opposite:
Leonard Bernstein, 1966.
Sony Music

Top:
Lenny at the age of four,
with his parents, Jennie and
Sam Bernstein.

Opposite:
Bernstein conducting the
Boston Symphony Orchestra
in Mahler's *Resurrection* Sym-
phony at Tanglewood,
Lenox, Massachusetts, July
1970.
Photograph by Heinz H.
Weissenstein, Whitestone

with generating the Mahler boom in America.

His conducting of works by classical composers such as Mozart and Haydn, often derided
in his earliest days, attracted more and more
praise as his career unfolded and he could relax a
little. "There is nothing Lenny can't do su-
premely well," an acquaintance remarked several
years ago, "if he doesn't try too hard."

The future Renaissance man of American
music was born in Lawrence, Massachusetts, on
August 25, 1918, the son of Samuel and Jennie
Resnick Bernstein. A sister, Shirley, and a
brother, Burton, were born in the years following. His father, a beauty-supplies jobber who had
come to the United States from Russia as a boy,
wanted Leonard to take over the business when
he grew up. For many years the father resisted his
son's intention to be a musician.

The stories of how Leonard Bernstein discovered music became encrusted with legend over
the years, but all sources agree he was a prodigy.
Bernstein's own version was that when he was
ten years old his Aunt Clara, who was in the
middle of divorce proceedings, sent her upright
piano to the Bernstein home to be stored. The
child looked at it, hit the keys, and cried: "Ma, I
want lessons!"

By his own testimony, Bernstein did not hear
a live symphony orchestra until he was sixteen, a
late start for any musician, let alone a future
music director of the Philharmonic. Virgil
Thomson, while music critic of the *New York
Herald Tribune* in the 1940s, commented on
this:

*Whether Bernstein will become in time a tra-
ditional conductor or a highly personal one is
not easy to prophesy. He is a consecrated character, and his culture is considerable. It might
just come about, though, that, having to learn*
*the classic repertory the hard way, which is to
say after 15, he would throw his cultural begin-
nings away and build toward success on a sheer
talent for animation and personal projection. I
must say he worries us all a little bit.*

This concern for Bernstein's "talent for animation" and his penchant for "personal projection"
was to haunt the musician through much of his
career.

Economy of Motion Not His Virtue

As for "animation," that theme tended to
dominate much of the criticism Bernstein received as a conductor, particularly in his youthful days. Although he studied conducting in
Philadelphia at the Curtis Institute of Music
with Fritz Reiner, whose precise but tiny beat
was a trademark of his work, Bernstein's own
exuberant podium style seemed modeled more
on that of Serge Koussevitzky, the Boston Symphony's music director. The neophyte maestro
churned his arms about in accordance with
some inner message, largely ignoring the clear,
semaphoric techniques described in textbooks.
Often, in moments of excitement, he would
leave the podium entirely, rising like a rocket,
arms flung aloft in indication of triumphal
climax.

So animated was Bernstein's conducting style
early in his career that it could cause problems.
At his first rehearsal for a guest appearance with
the Saint Louis Symphony, his initial downbeat
so startled the musicians that they simply looked
at him in amazement and failed to make a
sound.

Like another prodigally gifted American
artist, George Gershwin, Bernstein divided his
affections between the "serious" European tradition of concert music and the "popular" Ameri-

can brand. Like Gershwin, he was at home in jazz, boogie-woogie, and the clichés of Tin Pan Alley, but he far outstripped his predecessor in general musical culture.

In school, he immersed himself in almost every subject, but outside he lived for the piano. "When I went to a party," Bernstein once recalled, "I just ran for the piano as soon as I got in the door, and stayed there until they threw me out. It was as though I didn't exist without music."

In many aspects of his life and career, Bernstein was an embracer of diversity. The son of Jewish immigrants, he retained a lifelong respect for Hebrew and Jewish culture. His *Jeremiah* and *Kaddish* symphonies and several other works were founded on the Old Testament. But he also acquired a deep respect for Roman Catholicism, which was reflected in his *Mass*, written in 1971 for the opening of the John F. Kennedy Center for the Performing Arts in Washington, D.C.

Such diversity was apparent in other aspects of his music as well. His choral compositions include not only songs in Hebrew but also *Harvard Songs: Dedication and Lonely Men of Harvard.* He was graduated in 1939 from Harvard, where he had studied composition with Walter Piston and Edward Burlingame Hill.

A sense of his origins, however, remained strong. Koussevitzky proclaimed him a genius and probably future musical director of the Boston Symphony Orchestra—"The boy is a new Koussevitzky, a reincarnation!"—but the older conductor urged Bernstein to improve his chances for success by changing his name. The young musician replied: "I'll do it as Bernstein or not at all!"

He pronounced the name in the German way, as BERN-stine, and could no more abide the pronunciation BERN-steen than he could enjoy being called "Lenny" by casual acquaintances. In a sense, he was in lifelong flight from Lenny Bernstein, from being treated as the raffish ordinary guy that the nickname seemed to suggest. Although some elder members of the New York Philharmonic never stopped calling him Lenny, Bernstein lived down the nickname, and in his later years heard himself addressed almost reverentially as "Maestro" in the world's music capitals. The man who had been patronized in print for many years as Glamourpuss or Wunderkind of the Western World or Pinup Boy of the Podium became a favorite in Vienna both as conductor and as accompanist for such lieder specialists as Dietrich Fischer-Dieskau and Christa Ludwig.

Fame brought the usual honorary degrees, and honors far beyond the usual. Not only did he conduct at La Scala in Milan, at the Metropolitan Opera in New York, and at the Staatsoper in Vienna, but he was also invited in 1973 to be Harvard's Charles Eliot Norton Professor of Poetry, lecturing on linguistics as applied to musical analysis. The distinction had previously been conferred on Robert Frost, T. S. Eliot, Igor Stravinsky, Aaron Copland, and Paul Hindemith. Typically, Bernstein's Harvard performance was greeted with a mingling of critical raves and boos.

Harvard played an important part in Bernstein's rise, providing him with a pinch of Brahminism. The boy whose bar mitzvah was held at Temple Mishkan Tefila had gone on to the elite Boston Latin School and graduated cum laude from Harvard with a Bachelor of Arts degree. During his last semester at Harvard, he organized and led a performance of Marc Blitzstein's *Cradle Will Rock,* a left-wing musical that had been banned in Massachusetts but that could not be proscribed within the academic walls. It was not his first fling as a producer. At age sixteen he had starred in his own

Above:
Conductor Serge Koussevitzky on the podium at Symphony Hall, Boston, in the mid-1930s.
Photograph by Egone Studio, Boston Symphony Orchestra Archives

Opposite:
Composer Marc Blitzstein and Bernstein reviewing a score, 1947.
Photograph by W. Eugene Smith, Life *Magazine,*
© *Time-Warner, Inc.*

Top:
Conductor Fritz Reiner, Bernstein's teacher at the Curtis Institute of Music, Philadelphia, from 1939 to 1941. Said to have a conservative style of conducting, Reiner is caught in a rare moment of exuberance.
New York Public Library, Music Division

Bottom:
American composers Elliott Carter, Aaron Copland, and Roy Harris, whose compositions were played by the New York Philharmonic during Bernstein's tenure as music director from 1958 to 1969.
New York Public Library, Music Division

production of *Carmen* at a summer camp, playing the title role alluringly dressed in a wig and black gown.

It was as a result of another schoolboy production at Camp Onota in the Berkshires that he met Adolph Green, with whom he later collaborated in several Broadway musicals. Bernstein was a camp counselor and theater director and Green was in Gilbert and Sullivan's *The Pirates of Penzance.*

An Unlikely Start for a Conductor

Subsequently, when Bernstein was out of a job in New York City, he looked up Adolph Green, moved in with him in his East Ninth Street apartment in Greenwich Village, and began playing the piano at the Village Vanguard for a group called the Revuers. The ensemble included Green, his musical comedy collaborator Betty Comden, and the actress Judy Holliday.

Bernstein met Aaron Copland at a New York dance recital in 1937 and through him came to know two other aspiring composers, Roy Harris and William Schuman. Admiring Bernstein's intuitive grasp of modern music and his phenomenal skill at playing complex orchestral scores on the piano, the three composers agreed that the young man should become a conductor. Dimitri Mitropoulos, the New York Philharmonic's music director, met Bernstein in the same year and added his vote to the consensus.

At that point, Bernstein "didn't know a baton from a tree trunk," as he later put it. Nevertheless, he had made up his mind. Because he had applied at the wrong time of the year and was turned down by the Juilliard School, he went to Philadelphia to audition for Fritz Reiner's conducting class at the Curtis Institute. The Hungarian maestro opened a score in the middle, put it on the piano stand, and

told Bernstein to play until he could recognize the piece. The aspiring conductor, who was having difficulty seeing the music because he was suffering from a hay-fever attack, nevertheless discerned that the work was the *Academic Festival* Overture by Brahms. He was accepted into Reiner's class.

At Curtis, he studied conducting with Reiner and piano with Isabella Vengerova. His earlier piano teachers included his neighbor Frieda Karp, Helen Coates, and Heinrich Gebhard. In 1940 he went to Tanglewood, where he studied at the Berkshire Music Center with Koussevitzky, who quickly adopted Bernstein and called him "Lenyushka."

In later years, Bernstein prided himself on having retained the respect and friendship of both Koussevitzky and Reiner, who held virtually opposing ideas about what a conductor should do and how he should do it. But the famously irascible Reiner told his acquaintances a somewhat different story: "He didn't leave me for Koussevitzky—I threw him out."

In truth, not all of Bernstein's associations with elder colleagues were warm and collegial. In John Gruen's biography *The Private World of Leonard Bernstein,* published in 1968, Bernstein asserted that Artur Rodzinski had once pinned him against the wall of a dressing room, trying to choke him out of jealousy over the young assistant's flair for publicity. But according to Bernstein, Rodzinski had by this time become somewhat peculiar: he always carried a gun in his back pocket, for instance, for psychological support when he faced the orchestra.

A Boycott Causes Stumble at the Start

It was Rodzinski, however, who gave Bernstein his chance to conduct the New York Philharmonic at a lean time when the young man was scraping

Conductor Dimitri Mitropoulos, signals an orchestra entrance from the piano. He and Bernstein met in 1937 when the Greek-born maestro was guest conductor of the Boston Symphony Orchestra and Bernstein was a student at Harvard. Dazzled by his playing of a Chopin Nocturne, Mitropoulos invited him to attend daily rehearsals for the concert (and, at a subsequent lunch, fed him an oyster and called him a "genius boy"). Mitropoulos's vigorous platform manner in conducting Robert Schumann's Second Symphony and, as his own soloist, leading a piano concerto from the keyboard, so impressed the young Harvard sophomore he began to dream of a conducting career.
Photograph by Fred Fehl, New York Public Library, Music Division

along as a musician in New York. When he was twenty-two Bernstein had been offered a guest-conducting engagement with the Boston Symphony Orchestra by Koussevitzky but had been forced to refuse. The American Federation of Musicians, to which Bernstein belonged, advised its members to boycott the Boston Symphony, the last of the major orchestras remaining unorganized. Bernstein tried to mark time by opening a teaching studio in Boston but, he later recalled, "nobody came."

That fall, he moved to New York, where he fared hardly better. Eventually he got a twenty-five-dollar-a-week job at Harms, Inc., a music publishing house, where his duties included listening to Coleman Hawkins and Earl ("Fatha") Hines and getting their jazz improvisations down on paper. He also wrote popular arrangements under the name of Lenny Amber (Bernstein in English).

The Philharmonic offer came without warning. Rodzinski had heard Bernstein conduct a rehearsal at Tanglewood, remembered the young man, and after an hour's discussion, hired him as an assistant for the 1943–44 season.

Assistant conductors by tradition do a great deal of assisting but not much conducting. Destiny had other plans for Leonard Bernstein, however, and when opportunity knocked one Sunday afternoon in 1943, he was ready to open the door. On November 14, Bruno Walter fell ill and could not conduct the Philharmonic. The young assistant took over the program, which included works by Schumann, Rósza, Strauss, and Wagner, and achieved a sensational success. Because the concert was broadcast over CBS Radio and a review appeared on the front page of *The New York Times* the next day, Leonard Bernstein's name suddenly became known throughout the country.

"Typical Lenny luck," some longtime Bernstein observers said. But Bernstein had given luck a hand: knowing that Walter was not feeling well, he studied the program's scores especially hard, just in case. At twenty-five, he had become a somebody in the symphonic world.

After that break, though he was still more than a decade away from becoming music director of the Philharmonic, Bernstein began to consolidate his gains. He put in three exciting but financially unproductive seasons (1945–48) as conductor of the New York City Symphony. He received no fee, and neither did the soloists.

Celebrity Comes in the Forties

In the late 1940s, Bernstein bloomed as a public figure. He came to be a familiar sight at the Russian Tea Room, at Lindy's, and at Reuben's. Newspaper columnists reported that he was a fan of boogie-woogie, the rumba, and the conga and that female admirers swooned when he stepped on the podium. Tallulah Bankhead once watched Bernstein conduct a Tanglewood rehearsal and said to him in her husky baritone: "Darling, I have gone mad over your back muscles. You must come and have dinner with me."

Just about everyone in those years wanted Bernstein. The United States Chamber of Commerce named him one of the outstanding men of the year, along with Nelson A. Rockefeller and John Hersey. His fans, it was reported, ripped at his clothes and attacked him in his car. Paramount tested him for the title part in a film about Tchaikovsky, but he was turned down, according to the conductor, because "my ears were too big." In fact, Leonard Bernstein looked the part of a pop idol with his strong profile and wavy black hair.

Musically, his career was on the upswing, too. In 1947 he conducted a complete Boston Symphony Orchestra concert as a guest, the first time

Above:
Artur Rodzinski, appointed conductor of the New York Philharmonic in 1943, named Bernstein his assistant conductor for the 1943–44 season.
New York Public Library, Music Division

Opposite:
First rehearsal with the New York City Symphony, 1945.
Photograph by Ruth Orkin

Top:
Composer Milton Babbitt, whose *Relata II* (1968), commissioned by the New York Philharmonic for its 125th Anniversary in 1967, was given its premiere performance by the orchestra under Bernstein's leadership.
New York Public Library, Music Division

Bottom:
Composer John Cage, student of Arnold Schoenberg in his early years, had become interested in chance as the governing quality of his compositions by the 1950s. When Bernstein conducted Cage's *Atlas eclipticalis* with the New York Philharmonic in February 1964, contact microphones were attached to each instrument. The sound was fed into an electronic system, from which it was distributed to six loudspeakers in various parts of the auditorium.

in Koussevitzky's twenty-two-year reign that any other conductor had been permitted to do so in Carnegie Hall. He served as musical adviser of the Israel Philharmonic Symphonic Orchestra for the 1948–49 season. He was a member of the Berkshire Music Center from 1948 and head of its orchestra and conducting departments from 1951. He served as professor of music at Brandeis University from 1951 to 1954. In 1953 Bernstein became the first American-born conductor to be engaged by La Scala, Italy's foremost opera house, located in Milan. He led a performance of Cherubini's *Medea* with Maria Callas in the title role.

During Mitropoulos's six-year tenure as music director of the Philharmonic, beginning in the 1951–52 season, Bernstein was a frequent guest conductor. In 1957–58, the two worked jointly as principal conductors of the orchestra. In October 1958, Bernstein was named music director.

The New York appointment would have been a severe test for any conductor. The orchestra's quality had gone down hill, its repertory had stagnated, and attendance had fallen off. Orchestra morale was low and still sinking. Bernstein leaped in with his customary brio and showmanship and his willingness to try new ideas.

He designated the Thursday evening concerts "Previews," at which he spoke informally to the audience about the music. He built his season around themes like "Schumann and the Romantic Movement" and "Keys to the Twentieth Century." Strange-sounding works by avant-garde composers like Elliott Carter, Milton Babbitt, Karlheinz Stockhausen, Gunther Schuller, and John Cage began to infiltrate the Philharmonic's programs. He took the orchestra on tours of Latin America, Europe, Japan, Alaska, and Canada.

It sometimes seemed that Bernstein could not possibly squeeze in one more engagement, one more social appearance. During one particularly busy stretch, he conducted twenty-five concerts in twenty-eight days. His conducting style accurately reflected his breathless race through life. Although in later years he toned down his choreographic manner, he remained one of the more consistently elevating conductors of his time. That irrepressible buoyancy sometimes led to trouble: in 1982 he fell off the stand in Houston while conducting Tchaikovsky and two years later repeated the frightening stunt while leading the Vienna Philharmonic in Chicago. The worst injury he suffered, however, was a bruise from the medallion he wore around his neck.

Throughout his Philharmonic years, he kept his ties with Broadway and the show-business friends he had made before he became an internationally acclaimed maestro. He had already written music for the musical version of *Peter Pan* (1950) and *The Lark*, a play starring Julie Harris (1955). For Hollywood, he wrote the score to *On the Waterfront* (1954). Musical successes on the stage had included *On the Town* (1944), *Wonderful Town* (1953), *Candide* (1956), and *West Side Story* (1957). Several of the stage works continue to thrive: in 1985 Bernstein conducted a quasi-operatic version of *West Side Story* (the cast included Kiri Te Kanawa and José Carreras) that pleased him immensely and introduced the work to a new generation of listeners.

Then there were the ballets *Fancy Free* (1944) and *Facsimile* (1946); the song cycles *I Hate Music* (1943) and *La Bonne Cuisine* (1947); the *Jeremiah*, *Age of Anxiety*, and *Kaddish* symphonies; the one-act opera *Trouble in Tahiti* (1950); Serenade for Violin and String Orchestra with

Bernstein decked out in a lei
as he conducts the New York
Philharmonic on tour, Ha-
waii, 1960.
Photograph by Jerry Y. Chong,
New York Philharmonic
Archives

Harp and Percussion (1954); and the *Chichester Psalms* (1965).

In the years after he left the music directorship of the Philharmonic to become the orchestra's laureate conductor, he returned to the theater. He created the ecumenical and controversial *Mass* and, with Jerome Robbins, the ballet *Dybbuk*. The latter work, staged by the New York City Ballet in 1974, was the fruit of an idea that Bernstein and Robbins had begun planning as early as 1948.

Bernstein's life took a turn toward greater stability in 1951 when he married the actress Felicia Montealegre Cohn. Her American father had been head of the American Smelting and Refining Company in Chile, and she had been sent to New York City to study the piano. After several years of off-and-on romance, they were married in Boston. They had three children: a daughter Jamie, a son Alexander Serge (named for Serge Koussevitzky), and a second daughter, Nina.

Bernstein and his wife began a "trial separation" after twenty-five years of marriage. They continued, however, to appear together in concerts, including a program in tribute to Alice Tully at Alice Tully Hall, in which Bernstein conducted Sir William Walton's *Facade* with his wife as one of the two narrators. Mrs. Bernstein died in 1978 after a long illness.

After leaving the music director's post with the Philharmonic in 1969, Bernstein hardly curtailed his frantic activities. He continued to guest-conduct, to record for Columbia Records, to conduct at the Metropolitan Opera, and to play the piano for lieder recitalists. His company, Amberson Productions, which he had formed with his friend Schuyler G. Chapin to handle his diverse interests, expanded into the new field of video cassettes.

Bernstein, a longtime Democrat and liberal, took a deep interest in politics and was a friend of the Kennedys. His *Mass* was dedicated to John F. Kennedy. Among guests at fund-raising parties in his apartment during the late 1960s were some of the leading civil-rights advocates of the period, a form of hospitality that inspired the writer Tom Wolfe to coin the term "radical chic." In his book *Radical Chic & Mau-Mauing the Flak Catchers*, Wolfe described a fund-raising party that Bernstein and his wife gave for the Black Panthers. During Bernstein's Philharmonic decade, the orchestra engaged its first black member, the violinist Sanford Allen.

Bernstein continued composing, if only in spurts. Late works included *Halil* (1981), *Jubilee Games* (1986), *Arias and Barcarolles* (1988), and a sequel to his opera *Trouble in Tahiti* entitled *A Quiet Place*. After its premiere in Houston in 1983, *A Quiet Place* was produced in a revised version at La Scala in Milan, the Kennedy Center in Washington, D.C., and the Staatsoper in Vienna.

Almost to the time of his death, Bernstein carried on a bewildering variety of activities, rushing about the world with the same tireless abandon that had characterized his life in the days when he was turning out a hit a season on Broadway.

But Broadway had changed by the time Bernstein's final theatrical score reached the Mark Hellinger Theater in March 1976. The long-awaited work that he and Alan Jay Lerner had composed, *1600 Pennsylvania Avenue*, closed after seven performances.

Not long afterward, he turned up in Israel, where the Israel Philharmonic was putting on a

Leonard Bernstein retrospective festival to celebrate the thirtieth anniversary of his debut on an Israeli podium. During a two-week period, his music was heard in concert halls, theaters, movie houses, and other auditoriums all over the country. In 1988, when he was seventy years old, Bernstein was named laureate conductor of the Israeli orchestra. That birthday year brought honors from all directions, but none seemed to gratify him more than the celebration staged for him on August 25, 1988, at the Tanglewood Festival, scene of so many triumphs early in his career. On November 14 of that year, to mark the forty-fifth anniversary of his New York Philharmonic conducting debut, he led the orchestra in an all-Bernstein concert.

Laurel wreaths continued to shower on him in his last decade. Elected to the American Academy and Institute of Arts and Letters in 1982, he was awarded the Academy's Gold Medal three years later. The city of Milan, home of La Scala, also gave him its Gold Medal.

A discordant note sounded in 1989 when he refused to accept a medal from the Bush Administration, apparently as a protest against what he regarded as censorship of an AIDS exhibition by the National Endowment for the Arts. Like many other artists and public figures, he contributed his services at concerts to benefit the fight against AIDS.

Bernstein's private life, long the subject of rumors in the musical world, became an open book in 1987 when his homosexuality was brought to wide public attention by author Joan Peyser in *Bernstein: A Biography.*

Far from slowing down as advanced age encroached, Bernstein seemed to accelerate. In 1989 he led a Christmas performance of Beethoven's Ninth Symphony in Berlin to celebrate the crumbling of the wall between East and West Germany. With typical flair, he substituted the word "Freiheit" ("Freedom") for the poet's "Freude" ("Joy") in the choral finale. The East German Government bestowed on him its Star of People's Friendship Medal.

Although he had reportedly refused an offer to return to the New York Philharmonic as music director, he agreed in 1990 to conduct six weeks of concerts for the next few seasons. Before collapsing from exhaustion that year in Japan, Bernstein had taken part in the Pacific Music Festival in Sapporo.

Late in his extraordinarily restless and fruitful life, Bernstein defended his early decision to spread himself over as many fields of endeavor as he could master. "I don't want to spend my life, as Toscanini did, studying and restudying the same fifty pieces of music," he wrote in *The New York Times.*

"It would," he continued, "bore me to death. I want to conduct. I want to play the piano. I want to write for Hollywood. I want to write symphonic music. I want to keep on trying to be, in the full sense of that wonderful word, a musician. I also want to teach. I want to write books and poetry. And I think I can still do justice to them all."

Above:
Bernstein receives a standing ovation after conducting Beethoven's Ninth Symphony in Berlin, December 25, 1989, celebrating the end of the Berlin Wall.
Associated Press Photograph

Opposite:
Bernstein conducting the Chicago Symphony Orchestra at Lincoln Center, New York, 1988.
Photograph by Henry Grossman

1940-48

THE NATURAL

At age twenty-one, enters Tanglewood conducting classes with Serge Koussevitzky in 1940. Composes first symphony, *Jeremiah*, in 1942. Writes a song cycle, *I Hate Music*, and makes celebrated New York Philharmonic conducting debut in 1943. Answering theater's call, writes the highly acclaimed ballet, *Fancy Free*, and the Broadway hit, *On the Town*, in 1944. From 1945 to 1948, conducts symphony orchestras at home and abroad. Asked by a New York newspaper which of his "different interests [he] will follow," replies: "Whatever seems most like fun at the time."

Right:
Bernstein and friends at Birdland, the New York jazz club, c. 1946. From left, Felicia Montealegre Cohn (the future Mrs. Bernstein), Leonard Bernstein, his sister Shirley, Oscar Levant, three unidentified men, friend and collaborator Adolph Green, clarinetist David Oppenheim, and an unidentified woman.
Photograph by Ruth Orkin

Opposite:
Leonard Bernstein, 1943.
Photograph by Heinz H. Weissenstein, Whitestone

Early Tanglewood Years

"Serge Koussevitzky and the Boston Symphony Orchestra had been presenting concerts for several summers at Tanglewood, an estate in the Berkshires bequeathed to the orchestra, and in 1940 Koussevitzky inaugurated the Berkshire Music Center as an adjunct to Tanglewood.

"According to his plan, worthy young musicians of various disciplines would study with a distinguished faculty in pleasant natural surroundings; student conductors—an elite few, supervised by Koussevitzky himself, would actually practice their skills with a full-size student orchestra.

"Thanks to strong letters of recommendation, Lenny was chosen as one of five student conductors in the inaugural year." So wrote Burton Bernstein, Lenny's younger brother, in *Family Matters: Sam, Jennie, and the Kids* (1982).

In a letter home, written soon after the young music student arrived at Tanglewood, he said: "I'm playing my first concert tomorrow night. Kouss gave me the hardest and longest number of all—the Second Symphony of Randall Thompson, 30 minutes long—a modern work—as my first performance . . . he is already making me a *great* conductor. . . . Please come up. All my love, Lenny."

Although the activities of Tanglewood were curtailed during the Second World War, Koussevitzky organized a benefit for the Red Cross at the Lenox Library in the summer of 1943. Jennie Tourel, internationally recog-

nized mezzo-soprano whose singing of *Carmen* at the Opéra-Comique in Paris had received high praise from critics, was invited to perform, and Koussevitzky asked Bernstein to accompany her. Then living in New York, Bernstein went to Tourel's apartment and, hearing her for the first time, announced: "You're good!" It was the beginning of a lifelong friendship. As an encore at the Lenox Library, she sang Bernstein's *I Hate Music: A Cycle of Five Kid Songs for Soprano and Piano*, its first performance.

Bernstein had met composer Aaron Copland at a New York dance recital in 1937. The date was November 14, Copland's birthday, and Bernstein attended a party at the composer's Empire Hotel apartment afterward. Bernstein commandeered the piano, playing Copland's *Piano Variations*, which captivated the composer and was the beginning of their friendship. He had recommended Bernstein to Koussevitzky for the first conducting class of 1940.

Top left:
Soprano Jennie Tourel and her accompanist Leonard Bernstein take a bow at the Lenox Library, Lenox, Massachusetts, August 25, 1943. *Photograph by Heinz H. Weissenstein, Whitestone*

Bottom left:
Bernstein receiving congratulations from Copland after a performance of the Berkshire Music Center Orchestra at Tanglewood, c. 1942. *Photograph by Heinz H. Weissenstein, Whitestone*

Opposite:
Composer Aaron Copland, Leonard Bernstein, and conductor Serge Koussevitzky at the closing ceremonies of the Berkshire Music Center, Tanglewood, c. 1941. *Photograph by Ruth Orkin*

Top left:
Bernstein (*far right*) and other junior members of the Tanglewood faculty gather with their guests on the steps of the Lenox Library, Lenox, Massachusetts, following a music forum, 1942. From left, Claudio Specs, student from Chile; composer, conductor, and pianist Lukas Foss, also on the junior faculty; composer Harold Shapero and Mrs. Shapero; Ruth Fine and her husband, composer Irving Fine, an assistant on the composition faculty; and Bernstein, of the conducting faculty. The lively music forums were organized and moderated by Copland, with Bernstein frequently sitting in at the piano.
Photograph by Ruth Orkin

Bottom left:
Bernstein receives the first piece of cake at Serge Koussevitzky's annual birthday celebration, July 26, 1942. Maestro Koussevitzky, founder of the Berkshire Music Center, was born in Russia in 1874, had lived and conducted in Paris, and arrived in the United States to become conductor of the Boston Symphony Orchestra in 1924. From the time Bernstein joined the first class at the Berkshire Music Center in 1940, Koussevitzky recognized his gift as a conductor.
Photograph by Ruth Orkin

Left:
A gathering of the Bernstein family and their friends, Tanglewood, 1946. From left, composer Marc Blitzstein, Bernstein's sister Shirley, his brother Burton, LB, his mother Jennie, and two students.

The first postwar session of the Berkshire Music Center was a gala year, with Bernstein conducting the premiere of Benjamin Britten's *Peter Grimes* (commissioned by Koussevitzky). Newly affluent, owing to the success of *On the Town*, Bernstein invited his brother and sister to spend the summer as his guests. Blitzstein, whose *Cradle Will Rock* Bernstein had produced at Harvard in the thirties, was spending the summer nearby.
Photograph by Ruth Orkin

Carroll & Graf Publishers, Inc.
New York

Bernstein's conducting style drew criticism throughout his life. In the early years, the famous conductors with whom he studied, Fritz Reiner, at the Curtis Institute of Music, Philadelphia, and Serge Koussevitzky, at the Berkshire Music Center, Tanglewood, in Massachusetts, fixed on one of its special characteristics: Bernstein worked without a baton, as he had seen Dimitri Mitropoulos do. "Something about the use of his hands must have excited Bernstein," wrote his biographer Joan Peyser. "He told his teachers what he believed to be true: that the conducting movements he made with his hands were more related to those at the piano than anything he could ever do with a baton."

In 1958, Robert Rice of *The New Yorker* declared: "His technique of communication with an orchestra involves the hands, the arms, the shoulders, the pelvis, and the knees, to say nothing of the forehead, the eyes, and the teeth, and until last week's Philharmonic concerts, he had rarely, if ever, been known to use a baton on the podium—apparently considering a stick supererogatory." Rice never explained this reversal to the baton.

Leaving aside the subject of stick/no stick, Harold Schonberg in *The New York Times* described the Bernstein style in 1979, using the adjectives "dramatic," "theatrical," "self-indulgent," even "vulgar," but added one thing it did have: "Life!"

Fancy Free, 1944

Bernstein composed the score for *Fancy Free,* a ballet about "three sailors on shore leave," in 1943–44. Choreographed by Jerome Robbins, his debut in that role, the work was an inspired evocation of the swing era, using the techniques of classical ballet and the syncopations of jazz. When it was premiered by Ballet Theater at the Metropolitan Opera House, New York, on April 18, 1944, the dance world went wild.

Robbins, already acclaimed for his dancing with Ballet Theater, had proposed the scenario to the company the previous year. When it was accepted in June, he enlisted Oliver Smith to design the set. Finding someone to write the music took longer, until Smith introduced him to a young composer-pianist-conductor named Lenny Bernstein who loved jazz and was interested in dance. A lively collaboration ensued.

"Bernstein began by composing the most difficult music possible, complex in rhythm, frantic in speed, and alien in style to anything that a ballet instrumentalist might conceivably have played before," wrote Agnes de Mille in her notes for the first recording of the score, in 1946. Robbins matched him, step for step, creating a technically demanding program for the three sailors and their girls.

Bernstein was engaged to conduct the premiere. According to de Mille, the Metropolitan Opera House, then located on West Thirty-ninth Street, was jammed with standees five

36

deep. The set drew a gasp and applause. "From the entrance of the sailors and the first measures of their brilliant, explosive, precise cavorting the audience sat up sharp in delighted attention." At the end, "there was a genuine ovation with approximately twenty curtains and a house cheering from its heart. . . . The next morning Robbins as well as Bernstein was a public man."

37

On the Town, 1944

New York, New York,
   it's a helluva town
The Bronx is up and
   the Battery's down.
The people ride in a
   hole in the ground.
New York, New York. It's
   a helluva town!
—From *On the Town*

New York, Dec. 28—
About once or twice a decade a reviewer gets an opportunity to heave his hat into the stratosphere, send up rockets, and in general start the sort of journalistic drooling over a musical comedy that puts an end to all adequate usage of superlatives. Last night at the Adelphi Theater, *On the Town* premiered. In a word—great.

With these words Jack O'Brian, drama editor for the Associated Press, announced to his readers nationwide that the latest collaborative effort of Leonard Bernstein, Jerome Robbins, and Oliver Smith had arrived on Broadway. On leave from the serious world of "art"—to the consternation of Koussevitzky and perhaps of the Ballet Theater management—the three collaborators on the ballet *Fancy Free* had created a full-scale musical comedy around their "three sailors on shore leave."

It was Smith's idea. Like Bernstein and Robbins, only twenty-five years old when *Fancy Free* premiered, Smith was branching out from set design to the role of producer—trying his sea legs, in a way, for the following year he would assume

joint directorship with Lucia Chase of Ballet Theater itself.

He had studied his new role well: He knew that every musical comedy must begin with a book, and at Bernstein's insistence the three collaborators called on Betty Comden and Adolph Green, Bernstein's friends from his earliest days in New York, where they had played the Village Vanguard with The Revuers, a cabaret comedy act.

The five Broadway greenhorns needed a good director. Lawrence Langner of the Theater Guild fell asleep during the audition and Elia Kazan turned it down. Next, wrote Joan Peyser in her Bernstein biography, "they brought it to George Abbott, the hottest director on Broadway and the man responsible for a hit show called *On Your Toes.*" Abbott, a great ballet enthusiast, had seen *Fancy Free,* and he said: "I like the smell of this—let's do it tomorrow."

After the show opened on December 28, 1944, Louis Kronenberger of the progressive newspaper *PM* wrote: "*On the Town* is not only much the best musical of the year, it is one of the freshest, gayest, liveliest musicals I have seen," and added: "It has its faults, but even they are engaging, for they are the faults of people trying to do something different, of people willing to take a chance."

Opposite:
On the Town, a musical comedy about the "three sailors on shore leave," opened on Broadway late in 1944. Bernstein wrote the score, Jerome Robbins choreographed the dances, and Betty Comden and Adolph Green (foreground) wrote the book and lyrics for the show. The Broadway debut of all four, *On the Town* was one of the happiest collaborations in theater history. The show was later turned into a Hollywood movie, produced by Metro-Goldwyn-Mayer in 1949.
Museum of the City of New York

Left top:
Scene from *On the Town.* Eager taxi driver Hildy Esterhazy (Nancy Walker), successful at last in luring Chip (Cris Alexander) to her apartment, sings "I Can Cook Too."
Photograph by Vandamm, New York Public Library, Theater Collection

Left bottom:
Scene from *On the Town.* Anthropologist Claire de Loon (Betty Comden) pours champagne for her new friend Ozzie (Adolph Green), as her fiancé, Judge Pitkin Bridgework (Robert Chisholm), plays butler (and second fiddle) in zebra-striped apron.
Photograph by Vandamm, New York Public Library, Theater Collection

Scene from *On the Town*.
Chip (Cris Alexander) reads
the guidebook to his friends
Ozzie and Gabey (Adolph
Green and John Battles) on
the subway to Manhattan.
*Photograph by Vandamm,
New York Public Library,
Theater Collection*

Top right:
Scene from *On the Town*.
The three sailors Chip,
Gabey, and Ozzie (Cris Al-
exander, John Battles, and
Adolph Green) leave the
Brooklyn Navy Yard at six
A.M. for twenty-four hours'
shore leave and sing "New
York, New York."
*Photograph by Vandamm,
courtesy of New York Public
Library, Theater Collection*

Bottom right:
Scene from *On the Town*. In
a fantasy sequence, Miss
Turnstiles (Sono Osato), a
woman in a subway poster,
comes to life dancing, surrounded by her beaus.
*New York Public Library,
Theater Collection*

Opposite:
Bernstein rehearsing for a
performance at Lewisohn
Stadium, New York, c. 1944.
In July of that year, he
played Ravel's Piano Con-
certo in G with his friend
and colleague from the
Curtis Institute of Music and
Tanglewood, Lukas Foss,
conducting.
Bettmann Archive

Summer concerts at Lewisohn Stadium had been a staple of New York life since 1918, when the great colonnaded amphitheater—modeled after one of the ancient stone ruins of Greece but in truth the City College athletic arena built in 1915—became the summer home of the New York Philharmonic-Symphony Society, as the orchestra was then known, and where it played a series of evening programs sponsored by the City of New York. Bernstein first conducted in the stadium, which held as many as 15,000 people, in the summer of 1944, after his highly successful debut with the New York Philharmonic at Carnegie Hall. Koussevitzky had recommended him to Fiorello H. La Guardia, under whose aegis as mayor of New York the city-run season was held.

On July 14 of that year, 10,500 people saw Bernstein lead the Mendelssohn Violin Concerto at the stadium with Nathan Milstein as soloist. *The New York Times* reported that Bernstein gave the soloist "able support" and that his interpretation of William Schuman's *American Festival* Overture was "filled with exuberance and vitality."

Other programs in that July series included Aaron Copland's *Our Town* Suite, which Bernstein had previously conducted with the Boston Pops Orchestra on May 7 and which Copland had dedicated to him, as well as Tchaikovsky's *Romeo and Juliet* and the Ravel Piano Concerto in G, in which Bernstein was piano soloist and Lukas Foss conducted.

Throughout the decade and into the fifties Bernstein would take part in this popular summer series, which come to an end in 1966 with the stadium's demolition in favor of academic expansion.

Celebrated American contralto Marian Anderson in concert with Bernstein at Lewisohn Stadium, New York, 1947.
Photograph by Ruth Orkin

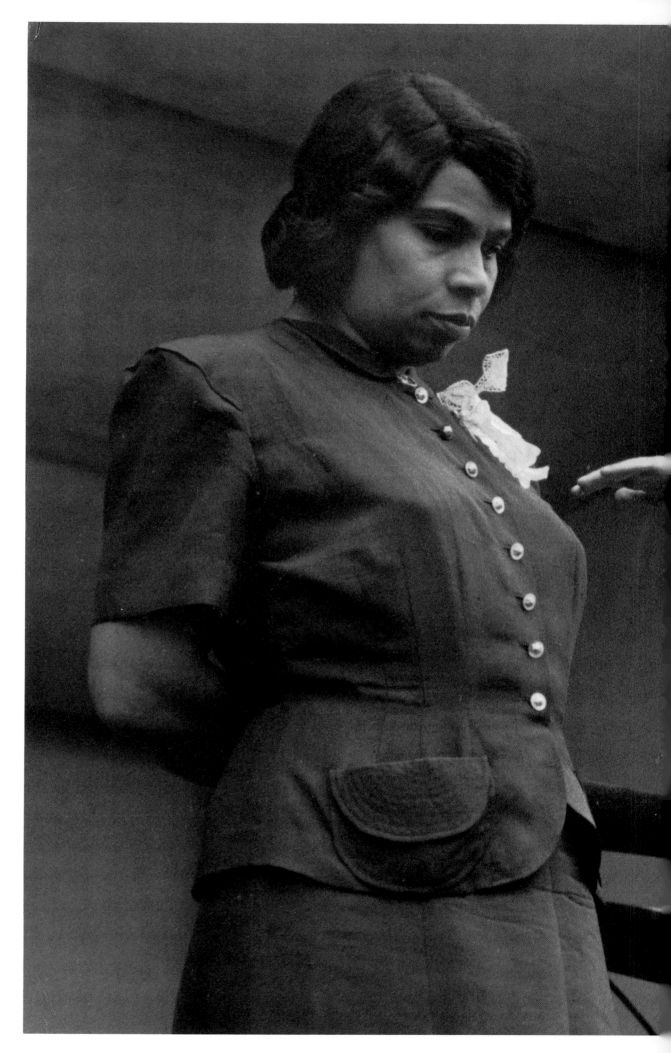

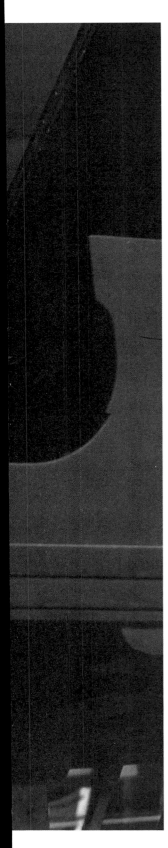

Left: Pianist William Kapell performed at Lewisohn Stadium, with Bernstein on the podium, in 1947. Kapell's career was tragically cut short when he died in a plane crash in 1953. *Right:* Bernstein conducting at the stadium, 1947.
Photographs by Ruth Orkin

47

Bernstein and Israel

In 1947 the United Nations voted for the partition of Palestine into Arab and Jewish states. When the State of Israel came into existence on May 14, 1948, Arab resistance was strong, and war broke out. In late September Bernstein left for Israel to conduct a series of concerts with the Palestine Philharmonic Orchestra (renamed the Israel Philharmonic) and to become its music director.

Joan Peyser, in *Bernstein: A Biography*, described the visit: "The official concerts—seven in eight days—took place in Jerusalem, Tel Aviv, and Haifa. But when Bernstein called for volunteers who wished to go farther, thirty-five musicians joined him, piled into two dusty buses, crossed the Negev Desert to Beersheba, the battle-scarred Old Testament town. There they gave the first symphony concert in its history. . . .

"Bernstein conducted a concert of Mozart, Beethoven, and Gershwin. While he was playing *Rhapsody in Blue*, his chair, balanced tenuously on a pile of flat rocks, began to slip. Bernstein stood up and continued to play while the first violinist adjusted the seat."

Top left:
Bernstein in Jerusalem, May 1947, where he conducted a series of concerts with the Palestine Philharmonic Orchestra. To his left is Golda Meir, the noted Zionist, who would serve as prime minister of Israel from 1969 to 1974.
Bettmann Archive

Bottom left:
Bernstein, center, with Rose Gershwin, mother of George Gershwin, whose *An American in Paris* Bernstein recorded in 1947 with RCA Victor.
Bettmann Archive

Opposite:
Bernstein at Beersheba, October 1948.
Bettmann Archive

1949-57

TEMPTATION

Broadway, ever beckoning, is held at bay. Continues to accept conducting engagements and to compose "serious" music: a second symphony, *The Age of Anxiety*, in 1949 and an opera, *Trouble in Tahiti*, in 1952. Then, challenged to write a Broadway musical in five weeks, succumbs: *Wonderful Town* opens in 1953. Soon after, writes *Candide*, opening in 1956. With *West Side Story*, in 1957, comes to full maturity in musical theater. Two new sirens: the burgeoning recording and broadcasting industries: "This old quasi-rabbinical instinct I had for teaching and explaining and verbalizing found a real paradise in the whole electronic world of television."

Left:
Newlyweds Felicia and Leonard Bernstein, 1951, playing a Bach Sonata on twin spinet pianos in their first New York apartment, located in the Osborne, across from Carnegie Hall.
Bettmann Archive

Opposite:
Bernstein, c. 1956, soon after signing his first recording contract with Columbia Records.
Sony Music

Top:
Poet W. H. Auden, at left, with Bernstein in January 1950. Bernstein had claimed Auden's long poem *The Age of Anxiety*, of 1946, as the inspiration for his Second Symphony, completed in 1949 and given the same title.

Auden's eclogue, a modern version of an ancient Greek poetic form in which shepherds converse, is a drama of three men and a woman meeting in a bar. A byword for mid-century literature, it was translated by Bernstein into a work for piano and orchestra with no sung or spoken text.

For the first performance, by the Boston Symphony Orchestra under the direction of Serge Koussevitzky on April 8, 1949, Bernstein was both piano soloist and author of the program notes. Speaking of his "extremely personal identification" with the poem, he added: "The pianist provides an almost autobiographical protagonist, set against an orchestral mirror in which he sees himself, analytical, in the modern ambience."

The Age of Anxiety was set to a ballet by Jerome Robbins for the New York City Ballet, and the work was premiered on February 26, 1950, just a month after this meeting of Bernstein and Auden.
Photograph by Ben Greenhaus, Boston Symphony Orchestra Archives

Bottom:
Bernstein at Tanglewood, August 1949, analyzing the score of *The Age of Anxiety* for a group of students as Artur Rodzinski observes, chin in hand.
Photograph by Howard S. Babbitt, Jr., courtesy Frank Driggs

53

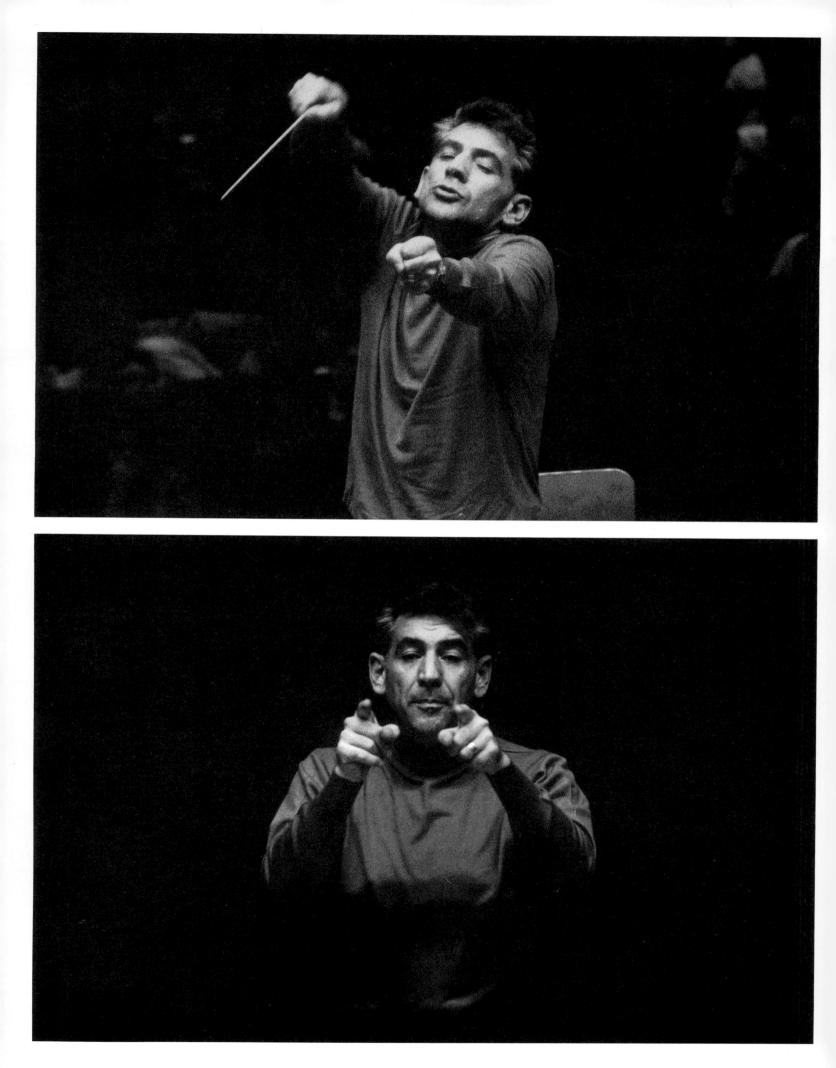

In Rehearsal

"Lenny is not a person it takes you six months to get to know," an old friend has said; practically no one— not even the musicians who work for him, or, for that matter, his doctor's office nurse—calls him anything but Lenny. Onstage, Bernstein is even less somber than he is off. His directions to an orchestra during rehearsals tend to be facetious, and are often phrased in pure Tin Pan Alleyese: "I want the next four bars *sehr* square," or "No! No! Not rallentando, just relaxo!
—Robert Rice, Profile,
   The New Yorker (1958)

Left:
Bernstein rehearsing with the Symphony of the Air at Carnegie Hall, 1950s.

Right:
Schmoozing with the musicians during the break.
Photographs by Jack Stager, Globe

Right:
Diva Maria Callas and Bernstein share an intimate moment at Teatro alla Scala, Milan, c. 1954, as Italian filmmaker Luchino Visconti casts a jaundiced eye from far right. They discuss their forthcoming collaboration in a production of Vincenzo Bellini's opera *La Sonnambula*, of 1831, directed by Visconti and opening in Milan on March 5, 1955.

Bernstein and Callas had met in 1953, when at the last minute he was invited by La Scala to conduct Luigi Cherubini's *Medea*, an obscure opera of 1797, which Callas had sung in Florence the season before. The first performance was on December 10. The score had been unknown to Bernstein, and the time to learn it was short—just six days. Nevertheless, in true Bernstein fashion he not only mastered it, but reorganized it and won bravos from the demanding Milanese audience for his lively performance. It was his first appearance in a major opera house and first venture outside the twentieth-century-opera repertory.
Archivio Fotografico, Teatro alla Scalla, courtesy Peter Kazaras

Opposite:
Bernstein, in a languid pose, waits in a greenroom, c. 1951, accompanied by his amanuensis and former piano teacher, Helen Coates.
Photograph by Ruth Orkin

Wonderful Town 1953

At the end of 1952, George Abbott called Comden and Green and said he had a book and Rosalind Russell, and he needed a score. "Can you get one together in five weeks?" he asked. They said they didn't know. He told them to call Bernstein and find out: "Is he yes or no?" Bernstein said yes.
—*Bernstein: A Biography,* by Joan Peyser, 1987

Right:
On January 19, 1953, the first out-of-town tryout of *Wonderful Town,* a musical comedy about New York, opened in New Haven to rave reviews. At the piano, Bernstein leads his collaborators in one of the songs; from left, lyricist Betty Comden, actress Rosalind Russell, co-lyricist Adolph Green, director George Abbott, and conductor Lehman Engel. After the New York opening on February 26, songs such as "Why, Oh Why, Oh Why-oh, Why Did I Ever Leave Ohio?" "Conversation Piece," "A Little Bit in Love," and "The Wrong Note Rag" were described by critic Louis Untermeyer as "both literate and lively."

It was based on the play *My Sister Eileen,* of 1940, by Jerome Chodorov and Joseph Fields, and that popular comedy in turn was taken from *New Yorker* stories by Ruth McKenney; she had written of her adventures in the big town with her younger, ingenuous sister, Eileen, fresh from Columbus, Ohio.

Olin Downes, music critic of *The New York Times,* was

more effusive: "This is an opera . . . made of dance, prattle and song and speed. . . . When the American opera created by a composer of the stature of the Wagners and Verdis of yore does materialize, it will owe more to the raciness of accent of our popular theater than to the efforts of our prideful emulators . . . of the tonal art of Bartók, Hindemith, and Stravinsky."
Photograph by Friedman-Abeles, Museum of the City of New York, Theater Collection

Right:
Scene from *Wonderful Town:* Ruth (Rosalind Russell), surrounded by the "hepcats of Greenwich Village," in "Swing," a Bernstein *hommage* to forties dance-band rhythms. In her odyssey, the girl from Ohio has taken a job at a Village nightclub, where the costume of the moment is a frilly gown with GAY SPOT emblazoned across the front.
Photograph by Vandamm, New York Public Library, Theater Collection

Scene from *Wonderful Town:*
Against a view of the New
York skyline by set designer
Raoul Pène du Bois, Vil-
lagers, Brazilian naval cadets,
and sisters Ruth and Eileen
sing "The Wrong Note Rag."
Photograph by Vandamm,
New York Public Library,
Theater Collection

It wasn't until 1954, when I got involved with television, that I realized the tremendous power of the [broadcast] medium, the power it could have in terms of music, and I got involved with it in a rather odd way. . . . One of the producers of *On the Town* was Paul Feigay. Now, in 1954 he was working with Robert Saudek in producing what was then known as *Omnibus*. Alistair Cooke, as narrator, was holding the whole thing together. It was a kind of magazine show with segments. And they had been planning one segment on Beethoven's Fifth Symphony, concentrating on the sketchbooks that he had written for that symphony. One day Paul Feigay called me and asked if I would be willing to do it. And I said I'd have a shot at it. . . .

We had the first page of the Beethoven Fifth, the whole score, painted in white on a black floor and we had musicians standing each on the designated line. Then I dismissed the ones that Beethoven had dismissed in his own mind. Because he begins the Fifth Symphony with only strings and clarinet, out went the flutes, oboes, horns, trumpets, leaving only the people who were relevant standing there. This made such an impression on people because it had this visual connotation of what I was saying . . . and it was unforgettable. . . .

I realized suddenly that . . . this old quasi-rabbinical instinct I had for teaching and explaining and verbalizing found a real paradise in the whole electronic world of television.

Transcription from *Reflections*, a film by Peter Rosen for the United States Information Agency, 1978, and published in *Bernstein: A Biography*, by Joan Peyser, 1987.

View of set for Bernstein's first television broadcast, "Beethoven's Fifth Symphony," *Omnibus*, Columbia Broadcasting System, November 14, 1954. Painted on the floor are the first thirteen bars of the score.
Photograph by Roy Stevens

Bernstein on Jazz

There were eighty-eight instrumentalists in the Philharmonic Orchestra that Bernstein conducted behind Louis Armstrong and his band at Lewisohn Stadium in the summer of 1955, a performance later described as *tout à fait exceptionnel.* "Jazz," Bernstein commented in an *Omnibus* television program the following fall, "is a very big word."

He gave the word more than its customary historical-sociological treatment in the program—called "The World of Jazz" and later presented as a chapter in his book *The Joy of Music*—focusing instead on what he described as the "musical innards" of the form. A surprise to viewers who had avoided the thought of jazz as "music"? Perhaps. Blue notes, not just flatted or "off key," are derived from the quarter-tone scale, "which comes straight from Africa, where quarter tones are everyday stuff." The rhythmic figures over the beat depend on syncopation: "A good way to understand syncopation might be to think of a heartbeat that goes along steadily and, at a moment of shock, misses a beat." Defending jazz, Bernstein equated its origins with that of similarly folk-derived European music. "Then there are those who argue that jazz is loud," he said. "But so are Sousa marches, and we don't hear complaints about them."

It may also have surprised Bernstein's viewers to learn, from America's leading interpreter of classical music, that what he described as the "new jazz" might prove to be

the beginning of "serious American music." In 1955, only a year after *Brown v. Board of Education,* this was, as he mentioned, a "startling conclusion." Though he didn't unequivocally add his name to the list of those who believed this, Bernstein did admit that "we have serious composers writing in the jazz idiom, and we have jazz musicians becoming serious composers."

"Perhaps," he added, "we've stumbled on a theory."
—Hettie Jones

Left:
Louis Armstrong, trumpet, and Edmund Hall, clarinet, in concert with Bernstein and the New York Philharmonic, summer 1955. Among their selections was the "St. Louis Blues," played to an audience that included its composer, the celebrated W. C. Handy, then more than eighty years old. The performance was filmed for *The Saga of Satchmo,* by Fred Friendly and Edward R. Murrow, released in 1957.

Right:
A Bernstein hug and a smiling orchestra greet Louis Armstrong, walking onstage for the rehearsal.
Photographs courtesy Frank Driggs

Candide 1956

Bernstein's score for *Candide*, called "a comic operetta based on Voltaire's satire" in the opening-night playbill, has survived some perilous times. When it was produced on Broadway in 1956—opening December 1 at the Martin Beck Theater—it was staged by eminent theater man Tyrone Guthrie and had lyrics by poet Richard Wilbur (with some help from John Latouche and Dorothy Parker). The book was by playwright Lillian Hellman.

Walter Kerr, theater critic for the *New York Herald-Tribune*, declared the production a "spectacular disaster," and Elliot Norton of the *Boston Record* drove the final nail in the coffin by declaring the Hellman book "clumsy and plodding." The first production ran for seventy-three performances.

Elliot Norton did say this of the first production: "Pictorially, *Candide* is magnificent, a brilliant pageant of bold and striking costumes by Irene Sharaff against shifting scenes of beauty from the palette of Oliver Smith," who designed the sets. "Musically," Norton continued, "this new show is also brilliant and memorable, rich in songs, in arias, and in great choral numbers by Leonard Bernstein: music that stirs and soothes and exhilarates."

In fact, the work did not die: imaginative productions by Gordon Davidson in Los Angeles, and Sheldon Patinkin in Chicago, were followed by a concert presentation at Philharmonic Hall

(now Avery Fisher Hall) on November 10, 1968, in which Madeleine Kahn played Cunegonde and Alan Arkin was Dr. Pangloss. A reincarnation in 1973 directed by Harold Prince with musical direction by John Mauceri (whose restructuring of the score to follow a new book by Hugh Wheeler was an invaluable contribution), successfully revised the work. Condensed, presented by a young cast whose average age, according to Prince, was twenty-two, it played first in the Chelsea Theater in Brooklyn and was moved in 1974 to the Broadway Theater in Manhattan, where it ran for two years. The acute ear of Stephen Sondheim's "adjustments" of some lyrics and addition of others provided a satirical edge that enhanced the score. An expanded "opera house" version followed, first presented by the New York City Opera in 1982.

And with such adventures, Bernstein "made his garden grow."

Scenes from original production of *Candide*, 1956:
Top left: Jesuit convent in Montevideo. *center left:* Raft sequence: from left, Dr. Pangloss (Max Adrian), Candide (Robert Rounseville), and Cunegonde (Barbara Cook). *Bottom left:* Buenos Aires *Opposite:* Venice gavotte: Dr. Pangloss (Max Adrian) and company.
New York Public Library Theater Collection

Soon after Bernstein signed his first contract with CBS Records in 1956, he set out on an ambitious recording schedule that accelerated when he was named a principal conductor of the New York Philharmonic the next year. In 1958, according to a discography by Paul Robinson, he had five recording sessions in the month of January alone, and on the date photographed recorded the Concerto No. 2 for Piano and Orchestra by Dmitri Shostakovich, *La Valse* by Maurice Ravel, and the *Manfred* Overture by Robert Schumann.

Bernstein established a pattern of recording works programmed in the regular Philharmonic season. On January 2, 1958, at Carnegie Hall, he conducted the first performance of the Shostakovich piano concerto in the Western Hemisphere and four days later entered the studio to record it.

On April 7, breaking a pattern, he recorded the Ravel Piano Concerto in G with the Columbia Symphony of the Air. He declared to Robert Rice in a 1958 interview in *The New Yorker* that the Ravel is a work he "owns," and, Rice continued, "he means that he is so familiar with the music, and so fond of it, that he could be roused from a sound sleep and led onto the stage in his pajamas, and give an acceptable performance." The Ravel appears on the reverse side of the Shostakovich recording; it was one of the outstanding releases of the decade.

Right:
Four views of a recording session, Columbia Records, Manhattan Center, New York, January 6, 1958. *Top left:* Bernstein conferring with the control room by telephone; *bottom left:* listening to a playback; *top right:* laying out a plan of action before recording begins; and *bottom right:* studying a score. *Photographs by Don Hunstein, Sony Music*

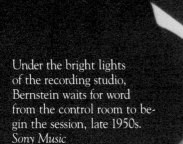

Under the bright lights of the recording studio, Bernstein waits for word from the control room to begin the session, late 1950s.
Sony Music

The disembodied arm of the
conductor leads the soloists
from the control room,
late 1950s.
*Photograph by Bruce
Davidson, Magnum*

West Side Story 1957

Bernstein was first presented with the idea of doing a modern version of Shakespeare's *Romeo and Juliet* by Jerome Robbins in 1949, but it took over six years before Bernstein, Robbins, and playwright Arthur Laurents actually got down to work on the project, August 1955. A twenty-five year old composer-lyricist named Stephen Sondheim was hired in November to collaborate with Bernstein on the lyrics, and work began in earnest.

Dramatizing the conflict between what Laurents described as "a Puerto Rican gang and a polymorphous self-styled 'American gang' on Manhattan's Upper West Side, the musical play opened in New York at the Winter Garden on September 26, 1957. It was a triumph. Brooks Atkinson, in *The New York Times*, called Bernstein's score ". . . a harsh ballad of the city, taut, nervous and flaring, the melodies choked apprehensively, the rhythms wild, swift and deadly." Carol Lawrence and Larry Kert etched "Tonight" on the musical memory of America, and Chita Rivera, as Anita, stopped the show with her spirited rendition of "America."

Bernstein's music ranged the gamut of emotion and musical styles from lyrical love songs ("Maria") and vaudeville routines ("Gee, Officer Krupke") to complicated ensemble numbers such as the second act duet between Maria and Anita ("A Boy Like That") in which quite contradictory emotions with their own individual musical character

are expressed at the same time—a technique common in opera but novel for a Broadway musical. Bernstein's music for Robbins's balletic sequences takes on symphonic complexity without losing sight of the limitations of the theater orchestra. It is clear that Bernstein already knew how important his work on *West Side Story* might be for the development of the American musical theater when during tryouts he wrote his friend David Diamond. "It really does my heart good—because this show is my baby, my tragic music-comedy, whatever that is; and if it goes in New York as it has on the road, we will have proved something very big indeed, and maybe changed the face of the American musical theatre."
—*Eric Richards*

Top left:
Choreographer-director Jerome Robbins, second from left, rehearses the dancers in *West Side Story.*

Bottom left:
Bernstein conducts a chorus rehearsal with lyricist Stephen Sondheim assisting from the piano.
Photographs by Friedman-Abeles, Museum of the City of New York Theater Collection

Opposite:
Principal members of the production team: from left, producers Robert E. Griffiths and Harold Prince, choreographer-director Jerome Robbins, lyricist Stephen Sondheim, composer Bernstein, playwright Arthur Laurents, and three unidentified members of the group.
Photograph by Martha Swope

Top and opposite:
Scenes from *West Side Story:*
The Dance in the Gym.
Members of the Jets, the self-
styled "American" gang,
show their stuff in the
Robbins dances.

Left:
Scene from *West Side Story:*
On the Fire Escape ("To-
night"). Tony (Larry Kert), a
Polish-American and a
member of the Jets, ser-
enades Maria (Carol Law-
rence), whose brother
Bernardo leads the rival
Puerto Rican gang, the
Sharks.
*Photographs by Fred Fehl,
Museum of the City of New
York, Theater Collection*

Inset:
The Bernsteins *mère* and *père* pose with their children Alexander Serge Leonard, born in 1955, and Jamie Anne Maria, born 1952. The photograph, taken about 1957, was found among the Marc Blitzstein papers at the University of Wisconsin, in Madison. Blitzstein, family friend and a composer whose work was frequently conducted by Bernstein, was the godfather of Jamie. A second daughter, Nina Maria Felicia, was born in 1962. *Wisconsin Center for Film and Theater Research*

Leonard and Felicia Bernstein share a private joke during a recording session, 1956. The Bernsteins, who met in 1946, were married in 1951. *Photograph by Dan Weiner, Sony Music*

1958-69

THE PHILHARMONIC YEARS

Named a principal conductor of the New York Philharmonic in 1957, and a year later, music director, remaining with the orchestra through 1969. Inaugurates televised Young People's Concerts with the orchestra in 1958. Celebrates the Mahler Centennial in 1960; obsession with the composer grows throughout the decade. Writes a third symphony, *Kaddish* (from the Hebrew prayer for the dead), in 1963, as world politics and nuclear missiles lead to thoughts of last things: "O my Father: ancient, hallowed, lonely, disappointed Father: Betrayed and rejected Ruler of the Universe, . . . I want to pray. I want to say *Kaddish*. My own *Kaddish*. There may be no one to say it after me."

Right:
Bernstein in Warsaw, 1959, at the home of Frédéric Chopin, plays the composer's piano during the fall 1959 tour of Europe by the New York Philharmonic.
Photograph by Don Hunstein, Sony Music

Opposite:
Leonard Bernstein, 1968.
Photograph by Heinz H. Weissenstein, Whitestone

79

Young People's Concerts

What is any particular piece of music all about? For instance, what do you think this tune is about?

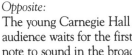

You will understand, I am sure, what my little daughter Jamie said when I played it for her. She said, "That's the Lone Ranger song, Hi-ho, Silver! Cowboys and bandits and horses and the Wild West . . ."

Well, I hate to disappoint her, and you, too, but it isn't about the Lone Ranger at all. It's about notes: C's and A's and F's and even F sharps and E flats. No matter what stories people tell you about what music means, forget them. Stories are not what the music means. Music just *is*. It's a lot of beautiful notes and sounds put together so well that we get pleasure out of hearing them. So when we ask, "What does it *mean*, what does this piece of music mean?" we're asking a hard question. Let's do our best to answer it.

With those words, Bernstein began his first televised *Young People's Concert*, "What Does Music Mean?" aired by the Columbia Broadcasting System on January 18, 1958. It was the first of fifty-three programs for children in which he appeared with the New York Philharmonic between 1958 and 1972. Many of his scripts were published in *Leonard Bernstein's Young People's Concerts for Reading and Listening*, 1961.

Top right:
Bernstein in the greenroom of Carnegie Hall with five young guests after a concert. *New York Philharmonic Archives*

Bottom right:
Wired for sound, Bernstein faces the audience as he conducts during a *Young People's Concerts* broadcast. *Wisconsin Center for Film and Theater Research*

Opposite:
The young Carnegie Hall audience waits for the first note to sound in the broadcast "Road to Paris," January 18, 1962, a program of music by George Gershwin, Ernest Bloch, and Manuel de Falla, each of whom worked in Paris during the early years of the century. Although the concerts were prerecorded, they took place before a live audience of children. And Bernstein wrote his own scripts.
The New York Times

Latin American Tour 1958

In April 1958, Bernstein and Dimitri Mitropoulos, then principal conductors of the New York Philharmonic, led the orchestra on a tour of twelve Latin American countries, playing thirty-nine concerts, of which Bernstein conducted twenty-eight. Slated to become music director of the group in the fall, he was the focus of considerable press coverage with photographers following his every move. His wife, Felicia, born in Costa Rica and a citizen of Chile, traveled with him during part of the tour, which coincided with President Nixon's celebrated visit to the continent. Nixon was booed, but the dynamic young conductor and the orchestra elicited cheers.

Left:
Bernstein rehearses for a performance in Lima.

Top right:
In the same city, Bernstein, center, receives a tour of the colonial art collection of Pedro de Osma.

Bottom right:
His horseplay amuses his Lima hosts. *Photographs New York Philharmonic Archives*

Top left:
Bernstein plants a big kiss on his wife, Felicia, who meets his plane in Argentina. She had preceded him to Buenos Aires, after visiting her family in Chile.

Center left:
Always a dandy, Bernstein in wrinkled linen and big shades waves to the airport crowds gathered for his arrival in Buenos Aires.

Bottom left:
Delighted fans scramble for autographs in the Argentinian city of Cordoba.

Top right:
Bernstein in Nehru jacket is greeted by the gentry of Maracaibo, Venezuela, in May.

Bottom right:
Long an asthma sufferer, Bernstein takes a whiff of oxygen before going onstage in the thin air of Bogota, Colombia.
Photographs courtesy New York Philharmonic Archives

Top left:
Composer Dmitri Shostakovich takes a bow at the conclusion of his Fifth Symphony, performed by the New York Philharmonic at a concert in the Tchaikovsky Conservatory, Moscow, in August 1959, with Bernstein on the podium.
Photograph by Don Hunstein, Sony Music

Bottom left:
The American conductor rehearses the orchestra in the Great Hall of the Tchaikovsky Conservatory, Moscow, during their three-week stay in Russia.
Photograph by Don Hunstein, Sony Music

Right, first and second from the top:
Reclusive Russian writer Boris Pasternak, third from left, out of official favor for his novel *Dr. Zhivago,* which had been awarded the Nobel Prize for Literature the year before, attends the Moscow concert of September 11 as the guest of Felicia Bernstein, and they join her husband in the greenroom at intermission. Pasternak is rewarded with the famous Bernstein hug.
Photographs by Don Hunstein, Sony Music

Right, third and fourth from the top:
At a Soviet Ministry of Culture reception for the orchestra on the evening before its final concert in Russia, honored guests include, from left, composer Dmitri Kabalevsky, New York Philharmonic assistant conductor Thomas Schippers, and Bernstein. To his left are Soviet Deputy Ministers of Culture Kuznezov and Danilov. Bernstein and two Philharmonic musicians, drummer Morris Lang and bass-player Robert Gladstone, reciprocate with some American jazz.
New York Philharmonic Archives

International Tour of 1959

Soon after Bernstein became music director of the New York Philharmonic in the fall of 1958, it was announced that President Eisenhower's Special International Program for Cultural Presentations had arranged a sweeping tour of the Middle East and Europe for the orchestra the following fall, and the trip would include nations behind the Iron Curtain. American relations with the Soviet Union were beginning to thaw under the rise of Nikita Khrushchev, and for Bernstein "to set foot in the land of his forebears as the esteemed American leader of a distinguished American orchestra was the stuff of historical fiction," wrote his brother Burton in *Family Matters*. Bernstein met his father's brother and nephew in Russia, and brought his father over for a reunion with them as well.

There were television broadcasts of the tour from Moscow and Venice. The one from Moscow is famed for the appearance on camera of Dmitri Shostakovich, after the playing of his Seventh Symphony, and an intermission visit with Russian novelist Boris Pasternak. Throughout the tour audiences were enthusiastic. The orchestra played American music by Barber, Bernstein, Copland, Diamond, Gershwin, Ives, and Piston, and Bernstein startled the Russians when he played Stravinsky's *Sacre du Printemps* and compared it to the Russian Revolution, a sacrilege in the Communist mind.

On the whole it was all a rousing success. Upon its return the orchestra played a concert at Constitution Hall in Washington, D.C., and recorded the Shostakovich Fifth, both to great acclaim.

Tour Itinerary

Left New York
August 3, 1959
Athens
August 5 and 6 (Bernstein conducting)
Baalbek
August 8 (Schippers) and 9 (Lipkin)
Istanbul
August 11 and 12 (Bernstein)
Salonika
August 13 (Bernstein)
Salzburg
August 16 (Bernstein)
Warsaw
August 18, 19, 20 (Bernstein)
Moscow
August 22, 23, 25, 26 (Bernstein)
Leningrad
August 28, 29, 30 (Bernstein) and August 31, September 1 and 2 (Schippers)
Kiev
September 4 and 5 (Schippers) and 7 (Bernstein)
Moscow
September 9 and 10 (Schippers) and 11 (Bernstein)
Scheveningen
September 13 (Bernstein)
Düsseldorf
September 15 (Schippers)
Essen
September 16 (Schippers)
Wiesbaden
September 17 (Schippers)
Luxembourg
September 18 (Schippers)
Paris
September 20 (Bernstein)
Basel
September 21 (Bernstein)
Munich
September 22 (Bernstein)
Belgrade
September 23 (Bernstein)
Zagreb
September 24 (Bernstein)
Venice
September 26 (Bernstein)
Milan
September 28 and 29 (Bernstein)
Hamburg
September 30 (Bernstein)
Berlin
October 1 (Bernstein)
Oslo
October 2 (Bernstein)
Helsinki
October 4 (Bernstein)
Turku
October 5 (Bernstein)
Stockholm
October 6 (Bernstein)
Göteborg
October 8 (Bernstein)
London
October 10 (Bernstein)
Arrive Washington, D.C.
October 12 (Bernstein)

Opposite:
Bernstein conducts a rehearsal in the amphitheater of Herodus Atticus, Athens, August 5, 1959, the first stop on a seventeen-nation tour of the Middle East and Europe by the New York Philharmonic.
Photograph by Don Hunstein, Sony Music.

This page:
Bernstein, third from left, and his wife Felicia on a walking tour of Zagreb, Yugoslavia, during the Philharmonic's 1959 tour.
New York Philharmonic Archives

Sightseeing in Russia

Top left:
The Bernsteins stroll down a busy Russian thoroughfare.

Center left:
He has his hair cut at the American trade fair, Sokolniki Park, Moscow.

Bottom left:
And his picture is taken in the Polaroid exhibit at the same fair.

Right:
In Kiev, where the orchestra plays three concerts, they visit one of the beautiful eighteenth-century churches.
Photographs by Don Hunstein, Sony Music

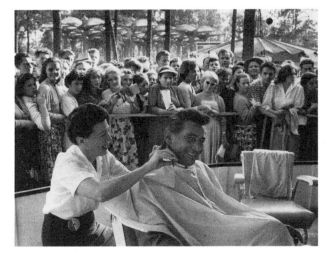

Opposite:
Bernstein conducting in Leningrad, August 1959.
New York Philharmonic Archives

89

On September 28, 1962, Philharmonic Hall, the keystone of the Lincoln Center complex opened in New York. It was among the first of the many cultural complexes that have sprung up across the country in intervening years, and Bernstein was there. It takes an Englishman to remind us New Yorkers of our origins: This hall of culture occupies, notes Peter Conrad, the very site of the tenements and cornerstores where *West Side Story* was born.

It was a night when music was the last thing on most minds. There was the subject of acoustics and Mrs. Kennedy's gown and of traffic and parties. But it was the night of the first "Live from Lincoln Center" broadcast. And Bernstein knew just what to do. He filled the stage with famous singers and played "sound bites" of pieces, and the broadcast was beamed to thousands nationwide. But trust Bernstein to redeem himself: His old friend Aaron Copland was commissioned to provide a piece for the opening, and despite its atonality, Bernstein played *Connotations for Orchestra* for all he was worth. "It can be noted," wrote Harold Schonberg in *The New York Times*, "that the New York Philharmonic sounded in brilliant form, and that Mr. Bernstein, buoyed by the occasion and by a program so admirably suited to his uninhibited personality, led the orchestra as an extension of himself."

Opening Night Program

Right:
Bernstein on the podium, Philharmonic Hall, at its inaugural concert.
Sony Music

Opposite:
View of Philharmonic Hall, opening night, September 23, 1962. Bernstein leads the audience, soloists, and choirs in the national anthem.
The New York Times

Bernstein and Falstaff

Bernstein made his first appearance at the Metropolitan Opera, New York, in 1964, when on March 6 he conducted Verdi's *Falstaff* in a production designed and directed by Franco Zeffirelli, the noted Italian stage director. According to Herman Krawitz, then assistant general manager of the Met, the two were "in tune." They brought new life to the charming old womanizer lifted by librettist Boito from Shakespeare's *Merry Wives of Windsor* and repatriated by him, in the words of writer Peter Conrad, "from Puritanical England to sensual Italy." By all accounts, Bernstein and Zeffirelli not only understood the librettist's—and Verdi's—intent, they gave Falstaff his *carta verde*, if that is the Italian for green card.

With a Bernstein twist: he concentrated on details of color, rhythm, precision, and clarity, and to the dismay of Krawitz asked for extra time from the musicians to achieve it. The results were so exceptional that even Harold Schonberg of the *Times* said: "From the second act he was a different director and *Falstaff* a different opera." After the ten performances at the Met in March–April 1964, Bernstein would go on to direct the opera at the Vienna State Opera in 1966.

Top left:
Mistress Ford (Gabriella Tucci), Dame Quickly (Regina Resnik), and Mistress Page (Rosalind Elias), in place for Act II, scene 2.

Top right:
Bernstein takes a curtain call with, from left, Rosalind Elias, Gabriella Tucci, Judith Raskin, Mario Sereni, Regina Resnik, and Luigi Alva.

Bottom:
Finale of *Falstaff,* opening-night performance, March 6, 1964.
Photographs by Beth Bergman

Opposite, top and bottom left:
Director Franco Zeffirelli demonstrates the gesture he's after for a weary Bernstein, his neck wrapped in a perspiration-soaked towel.

Opposite, top and bottom right:
Falstaff (Anselmo Colzani), pouring himself some life-giving ale.
Photographs by David Attie

Bernstein's television career burgeoned in this period, as in 1958 he not only inaugurated the televised *Young People's Concerts*, but began a new series for adults, called *Leonard Bernstein and the New York Philharmonic*, sponsored by Lincoln and Ford. Like its predecessor, the *Omnibus* series, it was produced by Robert Saudek. On this occasion, a broadcast of January 31, 1960, Canadian pianist Glenn Gould and composer Igor Stravinsky made their television debuts in a program called the "Creative Performer," with the composer leading the orchestra in his own *Firebird* Suite and Gould playing the first movement of the B Minor Concerto by Bach. Bernstein gave a lesson on the interpreter's importance to the life of the musical composition, leading the Philharmonic in excerpts from the Beethoven Third Symphony as well. Among other broadcasts in the series were the two programs from Moscow and Venice of 1959, and his investigation of the "Drama of *Carmen*," aired in 1962, a presage to his interpretation of the work with the Metropolitan Opera ten years later.

Four candid shots of "The Creative Performer," *Ford Presents Leonard Bernstein and the New York Philharmonic*, CBS Television, January 31, 1960.

Top left:
Bernstein adjusts Glenn Gould's tie before the performance begins.

Bottom left:
He confers with his guests, Gould and Igor Stravinsky, on details of the program.

Right:
Bernstein follows Gould's lead as they perform the Bach Piano Concerto in B Minor.

Neophyte television performer Stravinsky takes the overhead camera in his stride as he conducts the Philharmonic in his *Firebird* Suite.
Photographs by Roy Stevens

Top left and right:
Bernstein in Austrian jacket rehearses for a recording of Mozart's Piano Concerto No. 15 in B-flat Major with the Vienna Philharmonic, March 1966.

Bottom:
He discusses a passage in Mahler's *Das Lied von der Erde* with Dietrich Fischer-Dieskau as in April they prepare to record that work with the orchestra, as well.

Opposite:
View of the Grosser Saal, Musikverein, Vienna, where Bernstein is leading the Vienna Philharmonic in a performance of Mahler's *Das Lied von der Erde*, March 1966, with baritone Fischer-Dieskau and tenor James King as soloists, the first of Bernstein's many guest appearances with the orchestra.
Photographs by Elfriede Hanak

Vienna 1966

When Bernstein was invited to conduct Verdi's *Falstaff* at the Vienna State Opera in the spring of 1966, with Dietrich Fischer-Dieskau singing the title role, the Vienna Philharmonic, orchestra of the opera company, invited him to lead one of its weekend concert series in the elegant Grosser Saal of the Musikverein.

There the celebrated American guest elected to play a Mozart piano concerto, conducting from the piano, and to lead performances of Mahler's *Das Lied von der Erde*—"The Song of the Earth"—with baritone Fischer-Dieskau and tenor James King as soloists. It was a *gemütlich* experience. The significance of Bernstein's choice of composers, two of Austria's own—Mozart, Salzburg-born, who spent the last decade of his life in Vienna, and Mahler, born in Bohemia, but whose late nineteenth-century years as head of the Vienna opera company have been referred to as a "Golden Age"— could not have been lost on this music-loving city.

The significance of a Jew, and an American at that, being invited to conduct was not lost on Bernstein. Vienna, "the birthplace of Freud, Schoenberg, Wittgenstein . . . not to mention Mahler . . . had become a city with almost no Jews," he commented many years later, in an interview in *Rolling Stone*. But he added: "People ask me how I can go to Vienna and conduct the Philharmonic. Simply, it's because I love the way they love music. And love does a *lot* of things."

Leonard and Felicia Bernstein in their Park Avenue apartment with daughter, Jamie, and son, Alexander, c. 1960.
Photograph by Henri Cartier-Bresson, Magnum

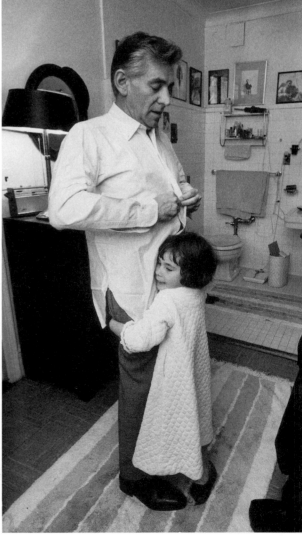

Opposite:
Left: Alexander Bernstein receives a tender good-bye before a performance; *top right:* Jamie Bernstein and her father enjoy a film at Expo '67 in Montreal; *bottom right:* Nina Bernstein grabs a hug as her father dresses for the day, 1967.
Photographs by Ken Heyman

Right:
The Bernstein family in Fairfield, Connecticut: Nina, Felicia, Jamie, Lenny, and Alexander, with their canine friend, 1967.
Photograph by Ken Heyman

In Canada
Leading the New York Philharmonic in Montreal, 1967,
during a Canadian tour,
where Mahler was again in
clear focus. *Photograph by
Ken Heyman*

Bernstein with his beloved
orchestra at Philharmonic
Hall, New York, toward the
end of the 1966–67 season.
Photograph by Ken Heyman

1970-79

ACCLAMATION

Conducts orchestras worldwide, in Paris, Vienna, Tokyo, Tel Aviv, and New York. In Vienna, celebrates Beethoven's Bicentennial in 1970. On Broadway, for America's Bicentennial in 1976, *1600 Pennsylvania Avenue* strikes a rare sour note; it closes in seven days. Composes *Mass*, commemorating the slain president, John F. Kennedy, in 1971. International stature as conductor grows—and even his severest critic, Harold C. Schonberg of *The New York Times*, writes of his Beethoven's Ninth, with the Vienna Philharmonic, in 1979: "The first movement . . . had explosive bursts of power that sounded like the world being born. . . . [The] ending was apocalyptic."

Right:
Gathered in an elegant, if appropriately gloomy, setting for a production meeting of *1600 Pennsylvania Avenue* are, clockwise from top left, composer Bernstein, author of book and lyrics Alan Jay Lerner, an unidentified party to the gloom, director Frank Corsaro, theatrical producer Robert Whitehead, two more unidentified participants, and a second producer, Roger Stevens. Lerner and Bernstein's Bicentennial tribute to the American Presidency, *1600 Pennsylvania Avenue* was dubbed "Upstairs-Downstairs at the White House" by one critic. Directed until the Washington tryout by Corsaro (Gilbert Moses and George

Faison replaced him), the musical opened in New York on May 4, 1976, and closed after seven performances.
Photograph by Henry Grossman

Opposite:
Bernstein, c. 1976.
Photograph by Henry Grossman

Bernstein in the orchestra pit, Metropolitan Opera, New York, September 1972, considers a question of emphasis appropriate for his conception of the Bizet opera.

Bernstein and Carmen 1972

When on September 26, 1972, Bernstein came to the Metropolitan Opera for the opening night of the season, his third and final engagement by the company, he was dealing with new material. While the vehicle was tried-and-true *Carmen*, it was something he had never conducted in its full state except for a summer-camp burlesque staged as a teenager.

There was a lot riding on this production: It was to inaugurate the post–Rudolf Bing era and to serve as a memorial to his appointed successor, the Swedish impresario-director Goeran Gentele who had been killed in an automobile accident the previous summer.

The production was importantly cast (Marilyn Horne and James Mc-Cracken). And it was to test the validity for this big theater, frequented by a tradition-bound public, of restoring the original Opéra-Comique spoken-text version (eliminating time-honored recitatives interpolated by Ernest Guiraud), as well as many previously suppressed musical paragraphs in the Georges Bizet score.

The conductor, unlike others involved with the production, had been privy to Gentele's intentions. Thus, he, as much as director Bodo Igesz, had to enlarge on the barely developed concept. And shape it he did, perhaps not so much by specifics of staging as by the enormous vigor and freshness he brought to the opera's text. Cuts, once opened, were ruthlessly evaluated, alterna-

tive passages weighed, and tempos and instrumental focus freshly appraised, with results that caused many among the supposedly *Carmen*-jaded musicians to wonder whether they indeed were listening to and playing that same familiar work.

Even more extraordinary was Bernstein's infusion of character into so many details of the musical framework. The pop-aria Toreador Song evolved as a portrait of preening Mediterranean pompousness. The catchy Chanson Bohemienne, for Carmen, her smuggler girl-friends, and corps de ballet, became an insistent, microscopically graduated intensification of abandon. The Act IV finale, no longer just an angry scene between mezzo and tenor, both tilting at each other until latter knifes former, became instead a musical dialogue about mockery, obtuseness, despair, insanity, and mesmerizing acceptance, and no one in the audience that fall night needed a roadmap to find out where one was. Bernstein set out to make a *Carmen* unlike any heard before and to make of this repertory staple a work no longer to be taken for granted. And in spite of the inevitable balance of strengths and weaknesses inherent in all lyric-stage undertakings, he succeeded brilliantly, leaving, fortunately, an original-cast recording (made only weeks after opening night) to let future generations know all about it.

—*Harvey E. Phillips*

Czech designer Josef Svoboda's radical backlit set for *Carmen*, Act I. *Photographs by Beth Bergman*

Tanglewood 1971

Right:
Conducting Beethoven's *Missa Solemnis* in the Tanglewood Shed on Sunday afternoon, July 25, 1971. The soloists, from left, are baritone Sherrill Milnes, tenor William Cochran, contralto Maureen Forrester, and soprano Phyllis Curtin.

Above: Perched at the tip of the makeshift podium, Bernstein rehearses the Tanglewood Festival Chorus for the *Missa Solemnis* performance.
Photographs by Heinz H. Weissenstein, Whitestone

Above:
Bernstein playing the shofar, or ram's horn, at a rehearsal for *Mass.*
Photograph by Don Hunstein, Sony Music

Top and bottom right:
Scenes from *Mass,* with singer Alan Titus as celebrant and dancer Judith Jamison as supplicant.
Photographs by Fletcher Drake

Opposite top:
Celebrant Alan Titus encircled by dancers, as Judith Jamison, following their movements, remains outside.
Photograph by Fletcher Drake

Opposite bottom:
Curtain call, with Bernstein in embroidered tallith, a symbolic garment in Jewish ritual.
UPI, Bettmann Archive

Mass, 1971

Mass, which opened the Opera House at the John F. Kennedy Center for the Performing Arts in Washington, D.C., on September 8, 1971, was composed at the request of the late president's widow. Subtitled "A Theater Piece for Singers, Players, and Dancers," the work involved more than two hundred performers, with not only strings, brass, and percussion, but also a variety of keyboards, organs, and electric guitars.

In addition to Bernstein's score, it featured choreography by Alvin Ailey and sets by Oliver Smith.

When asked why a Jew would be writing a Mass, Bernstein replied: "We have to educate ourselves," and his choice of a form with a connection to the Kennedy family, themselves Roman Catholic, tells only part of the story. Although *Mass* takes its exterior form from Catholic ritual, its music is highly secular, including elements of folk, rock, and the blues, and its stance is antiauthority as well as antiwar. Coming at a time of social unrest, when thousands had taken to the streets to protest the war in Vietnam, *Mass* seemed a show of support for such challenges; the priestly celebrant, in response to those who shout against God for not preventing war, tears off his vestments and smashes holy vessels.

Although many in the audience applauded at length, others were shocked, finding the work profoundly sacrilegious.

Cavalleria Rusticana, 1970

Right:
Bernstein rehearses the chorus for *Cavalleria Rusticana* by Pietro Mascagni, which he conducted at the Metropolitan Opera, New York, on January 8, 1970, in his second collaboration with Italian director and designer Franco Zeffirelli. Reviews of the first performance were unanimous in finding Bernstein's tempos too slow, which Zeffirelli later corroborated, saying they approached "self-indulgence." But Bernstein's stated intent was to pare away the buildup of "tradition" the opera had acquired over the generations. In that respect, wrote *Times* critic Harold Schonberg, "one heard details that normally are glossed over. And he has insisted that the chorus enunciate carefully. All this is to the good."

Mr. Zeffirelli's set, a super-realistic, magnificently recreated Sicilian hill town, was dominated by a church fronted by broad, massive steps.
Photograph by Lee Romero, The New York Times

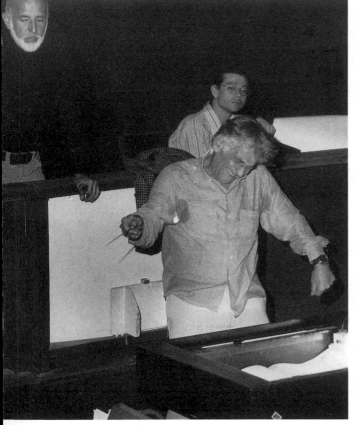

LB and Robbins Again

Above:
Two views of Bernstein in the pit at the New York State Theater during rehearsals. Jerome Robbins observes from top left.
The New York Times

Right:
Dancers Helgi Thomasson and Patricia McBride in a scene from *Dybbuk,* the ballet scored by Bernstein and choreographed for the New York City ballet by Jerome Robbins. Its first performance was May 16, 1974, at the New York State Theater, Lincoln Center, with the composer conducting.
Photograph by Martha Swope

In Tokyo 1974

Bernstein conducting the
New York Philharmonic in
NHK Hall, Tokyo, September 1974.
*Chubu Nippon Hosou Jig-
yobu, Tokyo, New York Phil-
harmonic Archives*

Left:
Two old Russians together:
a bearded Bernstein with
émigré cellist-conductor
Mstislav Rostropovich after a
concert with the Orchestre
National de France, Paris,
November 8, 1976.
Photograph by Jean Gaumy,
Magnum

Right:
Bernstein in closeup,
c. 1976. *Photograph by Gilda*
Hartmann, New York Philhar-
monic Archives

1980-90

THE MASTER

Teaches young conductors in the making at Tanglewood, Los Angeles, Sapporo and Schleswig-Holstein. Writes a full-length opera, *A Quiet Place*, in 1983–84. In 1986 indefatigably takes the cause of nuclear disarmament on a world tour, from Europe to Japan and back again. Submits happily in 1988 to a three-day celebration of his seventieth birthday; it is televised and broadcast around the globe. Continues to conduct with ever greater power, if less frequency, until a few months before his death. From *A Quiet Place:* "There is a garden: Come with me. There love will teach us harmony and grace. Then love will lead us to a quiet place."

We're neither pure nor wise
  nor good.
We'll do the best we
  know.
We'll build our house, and
  chop our wood.
And make our garden
  grow.
—Leonard Bernstein,
Candide, 1956

Opposite:
Bernstein at his Connecticut home, 1986.
Photograph by Henry Grossman

Right:
Accepting applause after the seventieth-birthday celebration at Tanglewood, August 1988.
Photograph by Walter H. Scott

Bernstein and Mahler

Mahler's Ninth Symphony became one of Bernstein's signature works in the later years. Here he conducts the Boston Symphony Orchestra at Tanglewood, Lenox, Massachusetts, July 29, 1979. *Photographs by Walter H. Scott*

A Quiet Place 1983–84

Views of *A Quiet Place*, second version, at Teatro alla Scala, Milan, 1984.
Top:
In the second act, Old Sam (Chester Ludgin) wanders into his suburban past with the help of his dead wife Dinah's diaries. A jazz trio in evening dress (Mark Thomsen, Louise Edeiken, and Kurt Ollmann), a fifties version of a Greek chorus, sings of the supposed pleasures of suburban life.

Bottom:
As the flashback continues, Young Sam (Julien Robbins) and Dinah (Diane Kesling) bicker over the breakfast table before he leaves for the office. The entire flashback originates in Bernstein's *Trouble in Tahiti*, a one-act opera of 1952, which was performed separately in the first production of *A Quiet Place* by the Houston Grand Opera, in 1983.

Top right:
At the curtain call, librettist Stephen Wadsworth is the first to receive a Bernstein hug. Applauding them are, from left, principal singers Chester Ludgin, Peter Kazaras, Beverly Morgan, and Robert Galbraith; production designer David Gropman; choreographer Grethe Holby; lighting designer Neil Peter Jampolis; principal singer Diane Kesling; conductor John Mauceri; principal singer Julien Robbins; and chorus master Mark Cogley.
Photographs by Grethe and Arthur Holby

Bottom:
In the third act, Junior (Robert Galbraith), far right, throws his mother's diary to the winds, and his sister Dede (Beverly Morgan), his father Old Sam (Chester Ludgin), and François (Peter Kazaras)—Dede's husband and Junior's former lover—attempt to recover the pages.

Production photographs by Lelli & Masotti, Archivio Fotografico, Teatro alla Scala, courtesy Peter Kazaras

Although much has been written about Lenny's multi-faceted talents as conductor, composer, and pianist, it is as a teacher that I remember him most vividly. Even after he had attained fame (even notoriety) and success unheard of in the classical music world, he remained passionately devoted to the development of young musicians. Each summer he returned to Tanglewood, where he'd studied in the forties, and in the last decade of his life he was instrumental in establishing similar institutions in Los Angeles, in Schleswig-Holstein in northern Germany, and in Sapporo, Japan. He led concerts around the world, where the first half of the program featured short pieces performed by young conducting students (all, of course, coached by Lenny). The Bernstein mystique, his aura, made every concert and every rehearsal an "event," no matter where in the world it was.

I am one of perhaps thousands who had the chance to play in an orchestra conducted by Lenny. That he had such a profound effect on my life and on the lives of so many other musicians is, more than any composition or recording, the strongest measure of his legacy.

In the years to come, history and memory will converge, and just as I still get a thrill whenever I hear an older musician's personal recollections of Pablo Casals, Arturo Toscanini or Glenn Gould, I will someday be able to tell my students that thanks to his absolute dedication to the future of his art, I once had the opportunity to make music with Leonard Bernstein.

—Gary Ginstling, Juilliard Master's Student

Editor's note: The writer is a clarinetist who worked with Bernstein at the Schleswig-Holstein Music Festival in 1988, and at Tanglewood in 1989 and 1990.

Opposite Top left and right:
Teaching at Tanglewood throughout the decade, Bernstein attracted a full house at every open rehearsal. At right, it's "perching room only" in the Barn as the Boston University Institute Orchestra rehearses. At left, he gives undivided attention to the teenage instrumentalists, who take part in special program for high school students.

Opposite Center left:
To the amusement of Seiji Ozawa, conductor of the Boston Symphony Orchestra, who observes from the piano, Maestro Bernstein hums the tune as he leads a conducting seminar at Seranak, the former Koussevitzky home on the Tanglewood grounds, in 1985.

Opposite Bottom:
Sans baton and attired in Roots sweatshirt, Bernstein rehearses the advanced students of the Tanglewood Music Center Orchestra for a public performance in the Shed, 1987.
Photographs by Walter H. Scott

Top left and right:
At left, Bernstein joins the Tanglewood Music Center Orchestra horn section to observe a conducting fellow in action, 1989. At right, he listens attentively as fellow Marin Alsop instructs the orchestra in a performance detail, also in 1989.
Photographs by Walter H. Scott

Bottom:
Returning to the Curtis Institute of Music, Philadelphia, where he studied between 1939 and 1941, Bernstein conducts the Symphony Orchestra on the occasion of the school's sixtieth anniversary, in April 1984.
Photograph by Neil Benson, Curtis Institute of Music

Vienna 1985

In Vienna, crowds fill the square in front of the State Opera to watch Bernstein on the giant television screen as he conducts the Hiroshima Peace Concert, August 11, 1985, commemorating those killed in the atomic bomb explosion forty years before.

It was the conclusion of a tour with the European Community Youth Orchestra on a "Journey for Peace" program, playing in Athens, Budapest, and Hiroshima (on the actual date, August 6), with Bernstein sharing conducting honors with Eiji Oue.

Photograph by Axel Zeininger

Right:

1. A hug from composer Jule Styne during ASCAP celebration of Bernstein's seventieth birthday, 1988.

2. With three young conductors, from left: Michael Morgan, associate conductor, Chicago Symphony; Michael Barrett, conductor and music director, Cathedral Symphony, Cathedral of St. John the Divine; and Michael Stern, associate conductor, Cleveland Symphony, 1986.

3. Jamie Bernstein, accompanied by her father, sings a selection from *West Side Story* at S.N.A.F.U. cabaret, 1980.

4. Rehearsing at the Kennedy Center for the sixtieth birthday celebration of Mstislav Rostropovich, 1987.

5. And the winner is . . . opera star Teresa Stratas after her Broadway debut in the musical *Rags*, 1986.

6. Listening to an unidentified violist at a rehearsal for the National Symphony Orchestra's Fourth of July concert, Washington, D.C., 1985.

7. With a beaming James Levine after the AIDS benefit concert, Music for Life, Carnegie Hall, 1987.

Photographs:
UPI/Bettmann: 1, 3, 4, 5, 6
Steve J. Sherman: 2, 7

1

2

3

4

5

6

7

1

2

3

4

5

133

LEONARD BERNSTEIN'S 70TH BIRTHDAY SONG

Stephen Sondheim

There once was a boy named Lenny
Whose talents were varied and many,
So many that he was inclined
Never to make up his mind.

In fact, he was so gifted
He seldom felt uplifted,
Just undefined.

Poor Lenny,
Ten gifts too many,
The curse of being versatile,
To show how bad the curse is
Will need a lot of verses
And take a little Weill:

★

Lenny made his mind up
When he was three,
He'd write a show, a ballet,
And a symphony.
But once the winds were tootled
And the first strings plucked,
He decided it was terrible—
He'd have to conduct.

Poor Lenny,
Time and again he
Complained, "I'm in this dreadful bind.
I feel for Leonardo—
God, genius is so hard—oh,
You cannot make up your mind."

★

Lenny made his mind up
When he was nine,
He'd be not only Bernstein,
He'd be Rubinstein.
"But just Rubinstein," he grumbled,
"That's like calling it quits,
When there's Hammerstein
And Wittgenstein
And Gertrude and Blitz."

Poor Lenny,
Knew there and then he
Might easily get oversteined.
From Ein to Ep to Jule
To Liechtenstein
    (pronounced "Liechtensteen")—no, truly,
He could not make up his mind.

★

Lenny made his mind up
At twenty-two
To do whatever Pinza
Or Astaire could do.
Though his voice was truly base,
He had the charm of a kid,
And if the dance floor didn't suit him,
The podium did.

Poor Lenny,
Wondering when he
Could show off all his gifts combined,
Began a TV feature.
It's best to be a teacher
When you can't make up your mind.

★

Lenny made his mind up
At twenty-eight
That marriage and a family
Would be just great.
But he had no time for weddings
Till a moment came
He was free between a tennis
And an anagrams game.

Poor Lenny,
Worse though, poor Jennie,
Who muttered all those years, resigned,
"I don't care if he picks a
Schlemozzle or a shiksa,
He should please make up his mind."

★

Lenny made his mind up
At forty-six
That maybe atonality
And rock would mix.
Though it certainly was serial,
With rhythm on top,
It had lots of snap and crackle,
But not enough pop.

Poor Lenny,
Pacing his den, he
Was worried he'd be left behind.
He mumbled, "How ironic,
Atonal is a tonic
When you can't make up your mind."

★

Lenny made his mind up
At seven-oh
To be a modern Renaissance
Like, man, you know.
And there's virtually nothing that
He hasn't done—
So get ready for his club act
At seventy-one.

Poet, pundit, seer,
Politician, skier,
Still at sea at three score ten.
Decked with every laurel
Lenny, here's the moral:
Do whatever pleases you and when.

Follow all your talents,
Don't attempt a balance,
Shower us with every kind.
Share your every vision.
Stick with indecision.

Don't make up,
You shouldn't make up,
You mustn't make up,
Don't ever make up—

Live another score and
Write another score and
Don't make up your mind!

Bernstein hugs his mother, Jennie Bernstein, as his aunt Dorothy Goldstein, looks on at his seventieth-birthday gala at Tanglewood, August 25, 1988.
Photograph by Angel Franco, The New York Times

Right:
No Bernstein performance was ordinary—Isaac Stern attests to that in his preface. But this one had greater importance than most. "It was forty-five years ago to the day since the astonishingly lithe, twenty-five-year-old assistant conductor had stepped up to the podium at Carnegie Hall to lead the New York Philharmonic for the first time, substituting for an ailing Bruno Walter," wrote Donal Henahan in *The New York Times* the day after these photographs were taken. "Now there stood Leonard Bernstein," he continued, "a white-haired, seventy-year-old patriarch, returning to conduct the Philharmonic in a concert of his own works. Need it be mentioned that nostalgia and sentimentality were also on the program?"

This concert took place on November 14, 1988, and it was one of several seventieth-birthday celebrations for the maestro. The Philharmonic played his *Chichester Psalms* of 1965, which, Henahan declared, "remains one of Bernstein's most irresistible works." It was entirely appropriate to select two early pieces, the Serenade for Solo Violin, Harp, Percussion and Strings (after Plato's *Symposium*), from 1954, and the even earlier Symphony No. 2 (*The Age of Anxiety,* after W. H. Auden's poem). It is the composer's lot, even on an auspicious occasion such as this, to encounter the critic's barbs. He found these performances not quite irresistible, and in the compositions quibbled with Bernstein's choosing to follow a "detailed program" in exploring the literary works. And so the evening of music got a B minus—"authoritative" for the performance itself, but "rambling," and "conveying too little sense of shape or purpose" for the works themselves. And so it goes.
*Photographs by
Steve J. Sherman*

Right:
In March 1990, Bernstein conducted Austrian composer Anton Bruckner's Ninth Symphony with the Vienna Philharmonic at Carnegie Hall, New York. Although better known for performing the work of Bruckner's countryman, Gustav Mahler, Bernstein was leading an ensemble utterly at home with the music. Analyzing the spiritual difference between the two composers for readers of *The New York Times* the following day, critic John Rockwell wrote: "Mahler strove, desperately and self-laceratingly, for faith; Bruckner smiled sweetly and unquestioningly in God's grace." Bernstein's performance achieved success, noted Rockwell, "in the supreme elegance and idiomatic naturalness of his playing." And, the critic added, "this was a great performance."
Photographs by Steve J. Sherman

Right:
Bernstein leaving the stage amid ovations at the conclusion of the annual Serge and Olga Koussevitzky Memorial Concert at Tanglewood on August 19, 1990, after conducting the Boston Symphony in a program that included Britten's "Four Sea Interludes" from *Peter Grimes*. In 1946, also at Tanglewood, Bernstein had conducted the American premiere of the work. This repeat performance, more than four decades later, was to be his last.

Opposite:
Conducting the last concert. *Photographs by Walter H. Scott*

CHRONOLOGY

1918
On August 25 birth of Leonard Bernstein in Lawrence, Massachusetts. He is the first child of Sam Bernstein, a Russian-Jewish immigrant who runs a barber-and-beauty-supplies business in Boston, and Jennie Bernstein, née Resnick, also Russian born. Officially named Louis, their first son is called Leonard by his parents and legally adopts this name when he turns sixteen.

1923
On October 23 birth of Shirley Anne Bernstein, Lenny's younger sister. Lenny's father goes into business for himself, founding the Samuel Bernstein Hair Company, which thrives when he obtains the New England franchise for the Frederics Permanent Wave Machine.

1928
Bernstein begins piano lessons with Frieda Karp, a neighbor's daughter, but his abilities soon surpass hers. He then takes lessons at the New England Conservatory of Music and, later, with Helen Coates and Heinrich Gebhard.

1932
Birth of Burton Bernstein, Lenny's only brother. Family moves to a spacious home in Newton, Massachusetts, and spends summers in Sharon, south of Boston, where Lenny organizes theatrical entertainments. He stages a *Carmen* spoof, playing the title roll himself in a wig supplied by the Samuel Bernstein Hair Company.

1935
Graduates from the prestigious Boston Latin School, where he proves a brilliant if undisciplined student. Enters Harvard University.

1937
Meets conductor Dimitri Mitropoulos, whose influence on Bernstein will lead him to a conducting career.

In the summer works as a music counselor at Camp Onota in the Berkshires; at a friend's suggestion, invites Adolph Green to play the Pirate King in the production of *The Pirates of Penzance* he is mounting. They become fast friends.

On November 14 meets composer Aaron Copland at an Anna Sokolow dance recital in New York and attends his birthday party that night.

1939
On May 27 stages Marc Blitzstein's proletarian opera *The Cradle Will Rock* at Harvard as it had first been done in New York two years before: no sets and no orchestra—just Bernstein at the piano (as Blitzstein himself had been), the characters singing their ballads and choruses from the audience. The composer attends the performance, later writing Bernstein that "it all packed a thrilling wallop for me—

second only to the original New York opening." The two develop a strong friendship lasting until Blitzstein's death in 1964.

On June 22 graduates cum laude from Harvard, where his teachers include Edward Burlingame Hill in orchestration, A. Tillman Merritt in harmony and counterpoint, Walter Piston in counterpoint and fugue, and David Prall (his special friend) in philosophy and aesthetics.

Spends first summer in New York. Shares a flat at 63 East 9 Street with Adolph Green and meets his friends Betty Comden, Judy Holliday, Alvin Hammer, and John Frank—a group called The Revuers that performs at Greenwich Village nightclubs. Bernstein sometimes sits in at the piano.

Enters the Curtis Institute of Music in Philadelphia, where he studies conducting with Fritz Reiner, piano with Isabelle Vengerova, orchestration with Randall Thompson, and score reading with Renée Longy. Excels in all subjects.

1940
Meets Serge Koussevitzky, conductor of the Boston Symphony Orchestra, who will become an important figure in Bernstein's life. Koussevitzky accepts him as a student at his new summer school, the Berkshire Music Center at Tanglewood.

1941
On May 3 receives diploma from Curtis and spends second summer at Tanglewood.

During fall and winter organizes a series of concerts at the Institute of Modern (now Contemporary) Art in Boston. Plays a two-piano recital of Stravinsky, Bernstein, and Mozart with composer Harold Shapero.

At the New England Conservatory of Music stages the Aaron Copland–Edwin Denby *Second Hurricane*, a children's opera, and casts it with young people from a local settlement house. Although the turnout is small, the production moves to the Sanders Theater at Harvard for several more performances; Bernstein hocks a girlfriend's emerald ring to pay for the theater rental.

1942
On April 21 premiere of Bernstein's Sonata for Clarinet and Piano, with clarinetist David Glazer, at Institute of Modern Art in Boston.

Answers summons from Boston draft board: classified 4-F (ineligible for military service) because of asthma condition.

Spends third summer at Tanglewood, now as Koussevitzky's assistant, and meets lifelong friend clarinetist David Oppenheim.

Above:
Isabelle Vengerova, Bernstein's piano teacher at the Curtis Institute of Music, Philadelphia.
Photograph by Blanche de Lorière, 1930, courtesy Nicolas Slonimsky

Opposite:
Bernstein, third from left, with classmates in orchestration at the Curtis Institute of Music, Philadelphia, 1939. Leading the class from the piano is Randall Thompson, then director of the Institute. To Bernstein's left is Hershy Kay, who later orchestrates several of Bernstein's Broadway scores.
Curtis Institute of Music, Philadelphia

In the fall moves to New York. Unable to find work as musician, takes job at Harms, Inc., a music publisher (at twenty-five dollars a week). His dance-band arrangements for the firm are published under his pseudonym, Lenny Amber ("Bernstein" translated from German to English).

On December 31 completes first symphony, *Jeremiah*, entering it in a competition sponsored by the New England Conservatory of Music. Although *Jeremiah* does not receive the prize, the work is published by Harms, Inc.

1943

During the winter and spring, living at the Hotel Chelsea, takes part in New York musical life; in February plays Copland's Piano Sonata at a Town Hall Music Forum; in March conducts Paul Bowles's *The Wind Remains* (a zarzuela based on a Federico García Lorca text) at the Museum of Modern Art; and in May plays a benefit, again at Town Hall. Still, his job at Harms, Inc., remains his major source of income.

In March meets composer Ned Rorem, another lifelong friend.

On August 24 accompanies mezzo-soprano Jennie Tourel at a song recital in Lenox, Massachusetts, a Red Cross benefit arranged by Koussevitzky. As an encore she sings Bernstein's *I Hate Music: A Cycle of Five Kid Songs*, its first performance. His friendship with Tourel begins at this meeting and continues until her death in 1973.

The next day, Bernstein's birthday, accepts invitation to be assistant conductor of the New York Philharmonic-Symphony Orchestra under Artur Rodzinski, who says: "I have gone through all the conductors I know in my mind, and I finally asked God whom I shall take and God says: 'Take Bernstein.'"

On November 14 Bruno Walter, guest conductor of the Philharmonic, becomes too ill to lead a Sunday afternoon program that is to be broadcast on CBS Radio. As Rodzinski is unavailable, Bernstein steps in, conducting Robert Schumann's *Manfred* overture, Miklós Rózsa's Theme, Variation, and Finale, Richard Strauss's *Don Quixote*, and a prelude from Richard Wagner's *Die Meistersinger*. *The New York Times* and the *New York Herald-Tribune* rave and Bernstein becomes an overnight success. Rodzinski is not pleased.

1944

On January 28 in Pittsburgh conducts premiere of *Jeremiah*, his Symphony No. 1, with the Pittsburgh Symphony Orchestra; Jennie Tourel sings the Lamentations.

On February 17 it is announced in *The New York Times* that Bernstein is relinquishing his duties as assistant conductor of the New York Philharmonic.

On February 18 makes conducting debut with the Boston Symphony Orchestra, which programs *Jeremiah* with Tourel as soloist, and Copland's *El Salón Mexico*. He repeats this program along with other works from the repertory when he conducts the Philharmonic the week of March 29.

On April 18 at the Metropolitan Opera House, New York, conducts premiere of *Fancy Free*, his score for a ballet choreographed by Jerome Robbins, and that evening Bernstein's reputation as a composer for the theater is established. The big success of the spring season, it is performed 161 times in the first year alone. The score is first recorded in 1946; blues singer Billie Holiday renders Bernstein's opening song, "Big Stuff," and the composer leads the orchestra.

On December 28 the musical comedy *On the Town*—with score by Bernstein and choreography by Robbins, book and lyrics by Betty Comden and Adolph Green, sets by Oliver Smith, direction by Broadway veteran George Abbott—opens at the Adelphi Theater in New York. A full-scale hit, it closes after 463 performances on February 2, 1946.

At year's end, *Jeremiah* is awarded a prize by the New York Music Critics Circle for the best new composition.

1945

On May 11 Max Helfman conducts the premiere of Bernstein's *Hashkiveinu*, a six-minute-long piece for tenor cantor, choir, and organ, at Park Avenue Synagogue, New York City.

On July 6 conducts his first concert of the season at Lewisohn Stadium, New York.

On August 25, Bernstein's twenty-seventh birthday, he is named director of the New York City Symphony, succeeding Leopold Stokowski, and holds the post for three seasons, performing at the City Center of Music and Drama.

On October 8 conducts first concert with New York City Symphony. His performance of works by Samuel Barber, Béla Bartók, Alban Berg, Marc Blitzstein, Carlos Chávez, David Diamond, Roy Harris, Paul Hindemith, Charles Ives, Darius Milhaud, Walter Piston, Igor Stravinsky, Randall Thompson, and Ralph Vaughan Williams attract younger, intellectual audiences to the twice-weekly concerts. Bernstein, along with such outstanding soloists as pianist Claudio Arrau and violinist Joseph Szigeti performs for free.

During the year he is paid for engagements with the major orchestras of Chicago, Cincinnati, Detroit, Pittsburgh, Rochester, and San Francisco.

1946

Meets Chilean actress and pianist Felicia Montealegre Cohn. Once a student of pianist Claudio Arrau, a countryman, she and Bernstein meet at the time of Arrau's perfor-

"All the News That's Fit to Print."

The New York Times.

LATE CITY EDITION
Cloudy and warmer today.
Rain tomorrow; colder at night.
Temperatures Yesterday—Max., 41; Min., 31
Sunrise, 7:48 A. M.; Sunset, 5:39 P. M.

Copyright, 1943, by The New York Times Company.

VOL. XCIII..No. 31,341. Entered as Second-Class Matter, Postoffice, New York, N. Y. NEW YORK, MONDAY, NOVEMBER 15, 1943. THREE CENTS NEW YORK CITY

BERLIN REPORTS RUSSIAN BREAK-THROUGH BY 30 DIVISIONS WITHIN THE DNIEPER BEND; BITTER FIGHTING CHECKS ALLIES IN ITALY

LACK MACHINERY DIRECTLY TO RAISE 'WHITE COLLAR' PAY

Federal Officials and Congress Stumped on Adjusting It to 'Little Steel' Formula

SPLIT ON SUBSIDY METHOD

Some Urge Price-Wage Control, While Others Seek WLB Provision for Unorganized

By LOUIS STARK
Special to THE NEW YORK TIMES.

WASHINGTON, Nov. 14—There is no immediate, direct method of adjusting the pay of about 15,000,000 clerical, white collar, unorganized employes to the 15 per cent "Little Steel" formula which applies to organized wage earners, according to Federal officials and legislators who were asked by THE NEW YORK TIMES for their views on the subject.

Some of those questioned, however, thought that an indirect approach could be made through a subsidy bill such as the one now before Congress, which is designed to keep prices of certain commodities from rising. Others, opposing subsidies as inflationary, made different suggestions but warned that they had no "panaceas."

William H. Davis, chairman of the War Labor Board, said that his solution would have been similar to that of Bernard Baruch: a stabilizing of wages and prices at the same time.

He told of receiving letters from persons complaining that they had not benefited by the 15 per cent formula, but said that he could not help them if they had no union to speak for them. Their only recourse, he said, were to "go out and get another job" or "tell the boss about it."

If "the boss" made a voluntary application for a wage adjustment it might be approved, he explained, but if he refused to act, the employe could do nothing because he could not apply to the board as an individual.

Price Ceilings as Protection

Chester Bowles, director of the Office of Price Administration, said that for the 15,000,000 whose pay envelopes had not appreciably increased and who normally live on a close budget, "each increase in the cost of living brings a lower standard of living."

"They have had no one to plead their cause in contrast with the cases presented by organized farmers and workers," he said.

"There is only one way to protect this group and all other American citizens from a higher cost of living and that is to stop prices from rising. That is what price ceilings are for.

"Citizens can help hold prices against wartime pressures by watching for ceiling prices when they shop and by refusing to pay a cent above the maximum legal price."

Frances Perkins, Secretary of Labor, felt that the subsidy bill was the practical approach to the problem.

"It is vitally necessary to hold the line on living costs and the white-collar people who have not benefited by wage increases can be helped if the subsidy program is adopted by Congress," she said.

Senator Robert F. Wagner of New York agreed that the subsidy method was the proper approach to alleviate the situation.

Byrd Stresses Wage-Price Plan

On the other hand, Senator Harry F. Byrd of Virginia, who favored the Baruch plan, declared that "wages and prices should have been stabilized at the beginning of the war."

"I am opposed to subsidies as a means of paying the farmer for his higher labor and other costs," he said.

"I don't know what the answer is. The WLB puts a lot of red tape in the way when employers want to raise wages. They have to fill out forms and then it takes months to get them approved.

"I know of a spraying machine manufacturer who took so long to get merit raises approved that his crucial employes left.

"To show you how organized employes benefit in wages, I found that the War Department approved wages for truck drivers which on a basis of eight hours a day, seven days a week would give them an annual income of $5,200. For the same period concrete mixers would get $7,200."

Senator Bennett C. Clark, Democrat, of Missouri, said that if he had a solution he would "shout it

Continued on Page Twenty-four

Cardinal Proposed To Head the Reich

By Cable to THE NEW YORK TIMES.

STOCKHOLM, Sweden, Nov. 14—A plan for one of Germany's Roman Catholic cardinals to be chosen to head the post-Hitler régime until the Reich found a democratic balance has been advanced in anti-Nazi circles at Berlin, according to advices received here today.

The proponents of this idea argue that the Allies would not approve of military rule or a monarchy, but that a stable government would be needed at once until democratically chosen leaders appeared.

Public support of a Catholic prelate as Reich Chancellor would be assured, they believe, from the fact that a recent survey showed 50 per cent of all Germans were now Roman Catholics, although before the war Catholics numbered only a third of the population.

LA GUARDIA GRANTS CURRAN TIME ON AIR

Offer for Next Sunday Follows Reading of Letter From Fly Calling Talk 'Accusatory'

Acting on the advice of James L. Fly, chairman of the Federal Communications Commission, Mayor La Guardia announced yesterday that Thomas J. Curran, chairman of the New York Republican Committee, would receive time during the Mayor's broadcast from City Hall next Sunday to reply to Mr. La Guardia's recent charge that the Republican party was responsible for the election of Thomas A. Aurelio to the Supreme Court.

The Mayor's charge was made during the weekly broadcast from City Hall on Nov. 7 over WNYC, the municipal radio station. Mr. Curran said that he would take advantage of the invitation to reply to such of the Mayor's statements as he would be unable to cover in a radio talk that he will make at 10:30 o'clock tonight over radio station WHN.

After the Mayor's broadcast of Nov. 7, Mr. Curran demanded time on yesterday's program from City Hall. The Mayor wrote to Mr. Fly for advice, enclosing copies of his own talk, of Mr. Curran's demand and of statements issued by Mr. Curran before and after the Nov. 7 broadcast. Mr. Fly's reply was on the Mayor's desk Saturday morning, but was given by the Mayor to an Associated Press reporter for safekeeping, to be returned unopened when yesterday's broadcast started.

"Political" Issue Sidestepped

In his letter Mr. Fly sidestepped the question of whether the Mayor's talk was "political." It was "accusatory," he wrote, and made serious charges and sought to place serious blame on the Republican organization. The Republican County Committee, he said, was entitled to express its views and the public to hear them.

"The time and facilities extended to the Republican organization," he declared, "should be no less desirable or effective than that enjoyed by you."

Specifically, Mr. Fly recommended that ten minutes of yesterday's broadcast or "at such other time as may be mutually arranged" be allowed for presentation of the Republican viewpoint.

Mayor La Guardia did not touch upon the Curran matter yesterday until he was well along in his weekly talk. Then he told of the controversy and of his appeal to Mr. Fly for advice, after which he read excerpts from his letter.

"Mr. Fly has replied," the Mayor

Continued on Page Fourteen

$2,500,000,000 COST SET FOR WAR RELIEF IN TENTATIVE PLANS

U. S. to Pay $1,000,000,000 to $1,500,000,000 and United Kingdom $625,000,000

QUOTA SYSTEM PROPOSED

Seen as Gaining Support From Congress—Our Share to Be Less Than Hoover Spent

By RUSSELL B. PORTER
Special to THE NEW YORK TIMES.

ATLANTIC CITY, N. J., Nov. 14—The Council of the United Nations Relief and Rehabilitation Administration (UNRRA) is working on a plan whereby the costs of the entire post-war relief and rehabilitation program, for which funds will have to be raised, may be kept down to $2,500,000,000, it was learned today.

Through a flexible formula whereby quotas are to be assigned to the non-invaded countries, it has been estimated that the United States share of the bill may run between $1,000,000,000 and $1,500,000,000 and that of the United Kingdom about $625,000,000. Being an invaded nation, Russia is not to pay anything for the relief of other peoples, according to this program, but she is expected to pay for the relief goods she herself receives.

This became known after an informal meeting in the Claridge Hotel by a group of advisers of Director General Herbert H. Lehman of UNRRA. Dr. Harry D. White, special assistant to Secretary of the Treasury Henry Morgenthau Jr., attended the meeting.

Seen Aid to Congress Action

Although those at the meeting declined to talk, it was disclosed in other quarters that the plan has been designed to solve the relief problem in such a way as to smooth its way through Congress. The first appropriation to be asked for is expected to be not more than $500,000,000 and possibly much less.

It was pointed out that the total cost of the entire world relief job to this country, if this plan prevails, would be only 40 to 60 per cent of the $2,500,000,000 that the United States spent on foreign relief after the last war through Herbert Hoover and the American Relief Administration, which he headed.

The United States would pay from 40 to 60 per cent of total monetary cost of relief this time, against about 25 per cent for the British, but it was pointed out that contribution from the Dominions would increase the amount for the British Empire or Commonwealth of Nations.

Several Quota Suggestions

A subcommittee headed by Dean Acheson, Assistant Secretary of State, United States member of the Council, and chairman of the present session, is to discuss the plan and make recommendations, which will come before the Council as a whole later on. If the Council accepts the plan, it will assign the quotas in the "community chest" manner, but it has no power to make assessments against any nation. The UNRRA agreement gives the Congress or legislative body of every country the right to accept or reject the quota assigned to it.

Several possible formulas have been suggested for determining the quota of each nation. One, which Mr. Lehman is said to favor, would take 1 per cent of the national income. This would vary

Continued on Page Eight

ATESSA IS CAPTURED

Victory by Eighth Army Is Sole Advance of Day on All Fronts

COUNTER-BLOWS BEATEN

Americans and Britons of Fifth Army Smash Germans—Air Action Increases

By MILTON BRACKER
By Wireless to THE NEW YORK TIMES.

ALGIERS, Nov. 14—There was a good deal of fighting on the Italian front yesterday but little progress was made.

The British Eighth Army ground forward three miles to capture Atessa and also sent patrols across the Sangro River for the usual exploratory work. But the advances of Lieut. Gen. Mark W. Clark's Fifth Army were strictly limited. German artillery and aviation demonstrated increased power.

In one of the day's sharpest clashes the American units of the Fifth Army smashed back elements of two German battalions northwest of Montaquilo. In the Mignano area, German guns crackled in a series of short, sharp counter-blows, but the Allies had no great trouble in battering them down.

In the air, light bombers and fighter-bombers concentrated on points within twenty-five miles of Isernia. Altogether, as many as sixty German fighters were seen over the battlefront, the greatest strength that the Germans have chosen to send up in many days. Nine enemy fighters were shot down in savage combats.

Evacuations Seen Near

From the Eighth Army's positions at Rionero, great columns of smoke were seen rising in the vicinity of Alfedena and Rocca Cinquemiglia, suggesting preparation to abandon these central points. This would not involve any appreciable sag in the Carigliano-Sangro line.

Alfedena is on the western spur of two highways into which the Boiano-Isernia-Rionero road divides four miles above Rionero. Rocca Cinquemiglia is seven and a half miles north and slightly west of Rionero and dominates the eastern spur. The Allies' progress beyond the junction along either prong would be serious to the enemy, because it would mean a threat to the trans-Italian road from Pescara to Rome. This intersects both spurs beyond Rionero at points approximately thirty-five miles above the junction. Both

Continued on Page Six

ENEMY INSTALLATIONS AFIRE ON BOUGAINVILLE

Smoke rises from Japanese posts on Torokina Point after an attack by dive bombers before our marines were sent ashore. Landing barges and a transport are seen in the foreground.
Associated Press Wirephoto

BADOGLIO TO RESIGN AFTER ROME FALLS

Premier Pledges Action When Capital Has Been Freed—King Retains Throne

By HERBERT L. MATTHEWS
By Wireless to THE NEW YORK TIMES.

AT PREMIER BADOGLIO'S HEADQUARTERS, In Italy, Nov. 13 (Delayed) — Premier Pietro Badoglio announced today that when Rome had been liberated he would cut himself off completely from politics.

Premier Badoglio has thus saved King Victor Emmanuel temporarily. The only thing he said today on the subject of the King's abdication was: "At the age of 17 I swore loyalty to the King, and I will continue to keep faith as long as I live."

Actually, there was never any question or any possibility of the King's abdication, despite reports to the contrary. There is a powerful demand for it in all political circles, but the King himself has always shown his determination to keep his throne. He is safe for the time being but that does not mean that he will be safe indefinitely.

Continued on Page Seven

Allies Deal Record Air Blow To New Guinea Madang Area

By The Associated Press.

ALLIED HEADQUARTERS IN THE SOUTHWEST PACIFIC, Monday, Nov. 15—Liberator and Mitchell bombers, following up a strafing raid by fighter planes, plastered Madang and near-by Alexishafen with 223 tons of bombs Saturday morning in the heaviest aerial assault yet thrown against the Japanese on New Guinea.

P-40 and P-39 fighters swept the air strips at Alexishafen shortly after dawn, at the expense of one craft shot down by intense anti-aircraft opposition. Then came waves of Liberators at medium height, followed by Mitchells at tree-top height, to give the enemy a thorough going over.

Towering fires were started in fuel and supply dumps at Alexishafen, where four Japanese planes were destroyed on the ground, and "the entire target area was covered with a heavy pall of smoke as our bombers left," Gen. MacArthur's communiqué said.

A strong force of P-47's and P-40's was on hand as a protective cover, but not a Japanese plane was in the air.

Since earlier attacks on the Wewak and Madang air strips kept the Japanese from aerial interference with the Australians' progress up the Markham and down the Ramu valleys, it was presumed that a giant assault such as this was intended to hamper the enemy's aerial supply of troops in forward areas.

The only heavier attack on bomb tonnage was the Oct. 12 raid on Rabaul, New Britain, which received 350 tons of explosives. The previous record tonnage on New Guinea was the 221 tons dropped on Satteiberg last Oct. 21.

There was no new word of the ground situation at Empress Augusta Bay, the Bougainville Island bridgehead secured by marines on Nov. 1 and reported by General MacArthur Saturday as having been extended.

A Catalina bomber that aimed

Continued on Page Three

NAZI CHUTISTS WIN LEROS STRONGHOLD

Enemy Seizes Narrow Waist of Island, Separating Two British Defense Bodies

By C. L. SULZBERGER
By Wireless to THE NEW YORK TIMES.

CAIRO, Egypt, Nov. 14—Fierce fighting continued today on the island of Leros between the British defenders and the German invasion force, with the British managing to drive the Nazis back on the range of hills on the northeastern peninsula of the island. The Germans enlarged their beachhead farther south.

Today's communiqué said:

"Heavy fighting continues on Leros, where the enemy has further reinforced his troops. In the northern sector our forces made local gains. In the central sector the enemy has somewhat improved his position but is being contained by our troops."

Already it would appear that the British forces have been cut from each other by the German thrust across the narrowest neck of the island, just west of the town of Leros. Due east of the town the German bridgehead on Point Bianco has been enlarged.

Thus, the town of Leros appears on the map to be threatened on two sides, while the defenders north and south of the neck bisecting the island at present are cut off from

Continued on Page Eight

BIG RETREAT LOOMS

Nazis Report Breaches From Zaporozhye to Krivoi Rog Sector

ZHITOMIR GAINS WIDENED

50 Villages Seized in 3-Pronged Push Toward Berdichev—Kerch Battle Unabated

By The Associated Press.

LONDON, Monday, Nov. 15—Berlin announced early today that nearly 500,000 Russian troops had broken through the German Dnieper River bend defenses in a new assault aimed at closing a gigantic trap on the huge Axis forces in the south. The Russian communiqué was silent on that point, but it did reveal that the northern Ukrainian Red Army had driven to within sixteen miles southeast of Korosten in a drive that scooped up fifty more villages.

The gains announced by the Russian communiqué and midnight supplement, recorded by the Soviet monitor, revealed that Gen. Nikolai F. Vatutin's armies were only twenty-one miles north of Berdichev, after having captured Pryazhev, six miles south of Zhitomir.

Korosten is the upper anchor of the last German north-south rail line short of the old Polish border and Berdichev is only sixty miles from the vital Lwow-Odessa line over which men and armament flow to the Germans facing disaster in lower Russia.

The Berlin broadcast, possibly preparing the homeland for a grand-scale retreat in the south, said thirty Red Army rifle divisions and numerous tank formations had snapped German lines between Zaporozhye and the area north and northwest of Krivoi Rog "at heavy cost" and that a big battle was continuing through the night.

Moscow's Silence Customary

Moscow's silence is customary at the unfolding of each new offensive, and the late German bulletin bore out previous German propaganda indications that a Nazi retreat to avoid encirclement in the south might be impending, if not under way.

The northern prong of General Vatutin's forces captured Chepovichi, a rail station on the Kiev-Warsaw line only sixteen miles southeast of Korosten.

The central units pushed on westward from captured Zhitomir toward Novograd-Volynski, near the Polish border, and also turned southward toward Berdichev.

The southern group battering toward Rumania ran into stiff opposition at Fastov, thirty-five miles southwest of Kiev, but beat off numerous enemy counter-attacks, the Soviet communiqué said. Five hundred Germans were killed in that sector and forty-eight tanks and sixty trucks destroyed.

In liberating Chepovichi and other towns and villages, the Russians said their troops had killed 1,600 Germans, captured thirty tanks and many prisoners, and freed 4,000 civilians being herded westward for "slave labor in Germany."

In the storming and capture of two enemy strong points near Kerch in the eastern Crimea, the bulletin said, the Russians killed 900 Germans. It reported that 1,820 more had died in the Pripet Marshes south of Rechitsa, where eleven more villages were seized by units outflanking Gomel.

Russian Pincers Closing

Hundreds of thousands of Germans are anchored in the Dnieper bend and along the Lower Dnieper. Three Russian armies moving against them form the southern pincers of the trap that General Vatutin's forces are creating in the northwest with their strides toward Poland and Rumania.

The capture of Zhitomir already had virtually split Germany's northern and southern Ukranian armies.

The horse-plus-armor sweep of the Russians toward the Polish and Rumanian borders moved ahead with about the same speed that had carried the Russians eighty-five miles from Kiev to Zhitomir in a week of steady fighting, and caused Muscovites to nickname General Vatutin "Lightning."

In the Crimea, where the Ger-

Continued on Page Two

Young Aide Leads Philharmonic, Steps In When Bruno Walter Is Ill

A nation-wide radio audience and several thousand persons in Carnegie Hall were treated to a dramatic musical event yesterday afternoon when the 25-year-old assistant conductor of the New York Philharmonic Symphony Orchestra, Leonard Bernstein, substituted on a few hours' notice for Bruno Walter, who had become ill, and led the orchestra through its entire program.

Enthusiastic applause greeted the performance of the youthful musician, who went through the ordeal with no signs of strain or nervousness. Artur Rodzinski, the orchestra's permanent conductor and musical director, who arrived at intermission time after motoring from his home in Stockbridge, Mass., declared the young man had "prodigious talent," adding that "we wish to give him every opportunity in the future."

Mr. Bernstein, appointed to his post at the beginning of the current season, was notified of Mr. Walter's illness in the morning by Bruno Zirato, assistant manager. Mr. Walter, who was said to be suffering from a stomach disorder, was to have been the guest conductor for the afternoon performance, broadcast over the Columbia network.

The young conductor, a native of Lawrence, Mass., and a Harvard graduate, had no opportunity for rehearsal before opening the program with Schumann's Overture to "Manfred." The program also included Rozsa's "Theme, Variations and Finale"; Strauss' "Don Quixote" and Wagner's Prelude to "Die Meistersinger."

Mr. Bernstein received hearty applause at the end of the Schumann overture, but was recalled four times when he concluded the Rozsa variations. The audience

Continued on Page Forty

War News Summarized

MONDAY, NOVEMBER 15, 1943

A German broadcast, as yet unconfirmed by the Soviet Government, announced that thirty Russian divisions had broken through the Nazi lines in the Dnieper Bend. Meanwhile other Russian armies, fanning out from Zhitomir, Ukraine rail junction, captured fifty more places and reached points sixteen miles from Korosten and twenty-three miles from Berdichev, the latter only sixty miles from the Odessa-Lwow railroad, the principal artery for the Germans in southern Russia. [1:8; map, P. 2.]

There was no official Washington comment on the statement by Soviet Ambassador Oumansky in Mexico that Russia would claim the Polish territory occupied under the Soviet-German pact of 1939. [3:8.]

The British Eighth Army captured Atessa in a three-mile push on the Adriatic end of the battle line in Italy, while General Clark's forces stopped severe counter-attacks northwest of Montaquilo. In air duels over the central and western fronts, nine German planes were shot down. [1:4; map, P. 6.]

Seventy-two-year-old Premier Badoglio, who arranged the Italian armistice and declared war on Germany, announced that he would resign when Rome was liberated. He pledged his loyalty to King Victor Emmanuel, whose reign now becomes virtually assured until the fall of Rome. [1:5.]

In the Aegean Sea battle, the Germans extended their beachhead on Leros Island, threatened the town of Leros from two sides and split the north-south British forces. The vital naval base was still in British hands. [1:7; map P. 8.]

In the Balkans the Partisans captured the Slavonian railroad junctions at Virovitica, where 500 Germans were captured, and Koprivnica, where 400 more Nazi soldiers surrendered. [8:1.]

British Mosquito bombers attacked Berlin in another "morale" assault and pounded other targets in western Germany. Last night marked the third anniversary of the Nazi "blitz" of Coventry, where 60,000 dwellings were hit. [10:5.]

The Germans were greatly alarmed in Jutland, Denmark, possible Allied invasion point, where they threatened to proclaim martial law to check widespread sabotage. [11:1.]

As a gesture of sympathy toward the Lebanese, whose Government leaders have been imprisoned by the French, Egyptian youth rioted and broke windows in the French Delegate headquarters in Cairo. The Egyptian Premier said he would ask the United Nations to aid in bringing about the release of the prisoners in Lebanon. [10:2.]

Allied bombers dropped 223 tons of explosives on Alexishafen and Madang, New Guinea, in a record attack there. [1:6-7.]

American submarines sank seven more Japanese vessels and damaged two others, bringing the total number of Japanese ships sunk or damaged by our submarines to 496. [1:6-7.]

Japanese Plane Transport Sunk As Our Submarines Bag 7 Ships

Special to THE NEW YORK TIMES.

WASHINGTON, Nov. 14—Continuing their assault against the life-lines of Japan's immense but shrinking empire, American submarines have sunk seven additional enemy vessels, including a plane transport, and damaged two others, the Navy Department reported today.

The Navy's communiqué did not explain the term plane transport, but it was believed that this vessel was a large freight ship carrying short-range Japanese fighter planes to the battle front in the southwest Pacific.

Besides the plane transport, the ships listed today as sunk were one large freighter, a medium-cargo transport and four medium freighters.

One large freighter and one medium freighter were damaged.

Total sinkings of Japanese ships by our submarines since the start of the war are now 346, with thirty-six probably sunk and 114 others damaged, or a total of 496 vessels.

WASHINGTON, Nov. 14 (AP)—Although the plane transport reported today as sunk was not further identified by the Navy and there was a question as to exactly what sort of ship was meant by that term, a spokesman carefully explained that it was not an aircraft carrier or a combat aircraft tender.

It might be either a regular merchant ship loaded with planes or a seaplane carrier. The Japanese have used float planes extensively both in the North and South Pacific. They are short range craft and to haul them about over the ocean the Japanese had special merchant-type ships equipped with cranes and catapults and presumably with supply and repair facili-

mance with the New York City Symphony. They become engaged, but Bernstein breaks off the engagement the following year.

In February becomes founding member of American–Soviet Music Society, promoting exchange of scores with Russian composers and sponsoring concerts of Russian music in New York.

On April 1 conducts the premiere of Blitzstein's *Airborne Symphony* with the New York City Symphony at City Center. Orson Welles plays the speaking role of Monitor (the "admonisher"). Eighty-five men of Robert Shaw's Collegiate Chorale perform the extensive choral section; baritone Walter Scheff and black tenor Charles Holland are soloists.

In the Spring, in Paris, meets Nadia Boulanger, famed teacher of Copland and other American composers in the American School at Fontainebleau.

On May 15 makes European conducting debut with the Czech Philharmonic in Prague, leading two concerts of American music at the First Prague Spring Festival. Eugene List is piano soloist.

On May 26 in New York conducts *Airborne* Symphony with the NBC Symphony of the Air, his first performance with that orchestra, of which Arturo Toscanini is music director. Blitzstein takes the role of Monitor. On October 30 Bernstein records *Airborne* for RCA Victor label with the Symphony of the Air, the RCA Victor Chorus, and Robert Shaw in the role of Monitor.

On July 4 conducts European premiere of *Fancy Free* with Ballet Theater at London's Covent Garden opera house.

On June 26 leads the London Philharmonic at Royal Albert Hall, where his conducting style is roundly criticized.

On August 6 leads American premiere of Benjamin Britten's opera *Peter Grimes* at Tanglewood with the composer and librettist Eric Crozier in attendance. Commissioned by Koussevitzky, the work is the high point of this first postwar season.

Conducts premiere of *Facsimile*, on October 24, performed by Ballet Theater at the Broadway Theater in New York City. Choreographed by Robbins and designed by Oliver Smith, it is the third collaboration (*Fancy Free* and *On the Town* were the first two) by this trio.

1947

In spring conducts Palestine Philharmonic Orchestra (later the Israel Philharmonic), playing nine concerts in Tel Aviv and more in Jerusalem and Haifa. It is the tenth anniversary season of the orchestra, founded in 1936 by German Jews fleeing Nazi Germany. These concerts mark the beginning of a long relationship with the orchestra that continues throughout his life.

After leaving Palestine conducts the Czech Philharmonic in Prague, the Radio Symphonique Orchestre (now Orchestre National) in Paris, the Brussels Philharmonic, and The Hague Orchestra in Scheveningen, Holland.

In the summer conducts Stadium Symphony (New York Philharmonic) at Lewisohn Stadium. Famed black contralto Marian Anderson is soloist in program of Handel arias and spirituals, sung before twenty thousand people.

In November publishes first article in *The New York Times*, "The Negro in Music," in which he deplores the absence of black musicians in American orchestras, a situation he attributes to the lack of training opportunities for blacks.

On November 24 and 25, in a second tribute to Blitzstein, conducts the New York City Symphony in a concert revival of *The Cradle Will Rock* at City Center. Howard da Silva plays Larry Foreman and directs the production. Will Geer, like da Silva a veteran of the original 1937 Federal Theater Project cast, recreates the role of Mr. Mister and, in a coup de théâtre, Shirley Booth plays Mrs. Mister. For critic Virgil Thomson, writing in the *New York Herald-Tribune*, *Cradle* remains, "ten years after its first New York success, one of the most charming creations of the American musical theater."

During the 1947–48 season of the New York City Symphony (his last) conducts Mahler's *Resurrection* Symphony, his first performance of a work by the composer. It is the central event of season.

1948

On May 10 conducts an orchestra made up of sixteen concentration camp survivors from Dachau—all that is left of an orchestra of sixty-five musicians—in Landsberg, Germany. Members of the Bavarian State Opera Orchestra, with whom he is rehearsing for a concert the next day, attend and bring him flowers.

Spends two months in Israel as music director and conductor of the Israel Philharmonic (renamed in May, when the State of Israel came into existence). Touring the country, he leads the orchestra in more than forty concerts in sixty days.

In the summer teaches at Tanglewood; meets British poet Stephen Spender.

1949

Completes his second symphony, *The Age of Anxiety*, based on W. H. Auden's poem of the same name. In April, only weeks after the score is complete, Koussevitzky conducts this work with Bernstein at the piano. The composer dedicates it to the aging maestro.

Teaches again at Tanglewood, and is guest conductor of the New York Philharmonic, Boston Symphony Orchestra,

Above:
Recording session of *The Airborne* Symphony by Marc Blitzstein, 1946. From left, Bernstein, recording engineer Dick Gilbert, Blitzstein, and choral conductor Robert Shaw.
Wisconsin Center for Film and Theater Research

Opposite:
Bernstein, top, pianist Eugene List, and violinist Carroll Glenn List en route to International *Music Festival, Prague, 1946.*
Bettmann Archive

145

Israel Philharmonic, Philadelphia Orchestra, and Pittsburgh Symphony.

Appointment of European conductor Charles Munch to post of music director, Boston Symphony Orchestra, is announced. As Koussevitzky's protégé, Bernstein had hoped for this appointment.

1950

On April 24 premiere of *Peter Pan*, starring Jean Arthur and Boris Karloff, at the Imperial Theater, New York, for which Bernstein writes lyrics and music. His return to Broadway is discouraged by Koussevitzky, who fears that Bernstein is jeopardizing his career as a "serious artist" by pursuing popular music and theater.

In the spring leaves on an extended conducting tour of Europe, taking him to England, Scotland, Holland, West Germany, Italy, and Ireland.

1951

On January 8 the Israel Philharmonic begins a tour of the United States with Bernstein and Koussevitzky sharing conducting honors.

On June 6 death of Koussevitzky.

On September 9 marries Felicia Montealegre Cohn at the Mishkan Tefilah synagogue in Newton, Massachusetts. Bernstein wears Koussevitzky's white suit and shoes, signaling his intent to follow in the conductor's path.

Appointed professor of music at Brandeis University, Waltham, Massachusetts, a position he holds through 1954.

1952

On June 12 Festival of Creative Arts at Brandeis, organized by Bernstein and his music faculty colleague Irving Fine, opens with premiere of Bernstein's one-act opera *Trouble in Tahiti*, conducted by the composer. It tells the tale of an unhappy suburban couple who are not in love. A trio comments on the story in pop music style, to the annoyance of most critics.

On June 14 the festival presents a concert performance of Kurt Weill's *The Threepenny Opera*, featuring Blitzstein's translation of the Bertolt Brecht libretto. Bernstein conducts, following the original Weill manuscript, and Lotte Lenya plays Jenny, the role she originated in Berlin in 1928. With some revisions, the critically praised work will open in New York two years later, in 1954, and run for 96 performances; after a year's hiatus it will reopen at the Theater de Lys, New York, to run for six years.

On August 8 two student performances of *Trouble in Tahiti* at Tanglewood are conducted by Seymour Lipkin and directed by Sarah Caldwell under the supervision of Boris Goldovsky, head of the opera program, and Bernstein.

On September 8 birth of daughter Jamie Anne Maria.

On November 16, *Trouble in Tahiti*, produced by the NBC Opera Company and directed by Kirk Browning, is broadcast on NBC-Television. Cast as Dinah and Sam are Beverly Wolff and David Atkinson, and the jazz trio is composed of Constance Brigham, Robert Kole, and William Harder.

1953

On February 21 the musical *Wonderful Town* opens to rave reviews at the Winter Garden Theater, New York. Bernstein produces the score in five weeks; Betty Comden and Adolph Green write the book and lyrics; George Abbott directs; Bernstein's friend, Lehman Engel, conducts and writes vocal arrangements. Rosalind Russell stars with verve and style. Koussevitzky would not approve, but Broadway welcomes Lenny back.

On June 13 conducts American premiere of *Les Mamelles de Tirésias*, a 1947 opera by Francis Poulenc, at second Brandeis festival.

On December 10 conducts Luigi Cherubini's opera *Medea* at La Scala in Milan, with Maria Callas in the title role. He is the first American to conduct at the celebrated opera house.

1954

On July 28 Columbia Pictures releases *On the Waterfront*, with score by Bernstein. Directed by Elia Kazan and produced by Sam Spiegel, the movie stars Marlon Brando and Eva Marie Saint. A year later the film wins the Academy Award for Best Picture, and Bernstein's Symphonic Suite from *On the Waterfront*, the notes lamentably "left on the dubbing-room floor" restored, is given its first performance at Tanglewood by the Boston Symphony Orchestra, with composer conducting.

On September 12 conducts premiere of his *Serenade* for Solo Violin, Harp, Percussion, and Strings, at La Fenice, Venice, with the Israel Philharmonic Orchestra. Violin soloist is Isaac Stern.

On November 14 begins television career with first of seven appearances on *Omnibus*; his series of tremendously successful lecture-demonstrations leads to the later *Young People's Concerts*. The first program, "Beethoven's Fifth Symphony," investigates the composer's sketches for the final work.

Bernstein signs a contract for six appearances with the Symphony of the Air in the 1955–56 season.

1955

In spring conducts two operas at La Scala in Milan: *La Sonnambula*, the Vincenzo Bellini vehicle for diva Maria

Callas, and Giacomo Puccini's *La Bohème*.

Remains in Europe five months. Leads the Israel Philharmonic on a European tour that takes the musicians to Germany for the first time since the Holocaust.

On July 7 birth of son, Alexander Serge Leonard.

Returns to Tanglewood.

On November 17 premiere of *The Lark*, an adaptation by Lillian Hellman of Jean Anouilh's play about Joan of Arc, for which Bernstein writes the incidental music. According to Brooks Atkinson in *The New York Times*, "Leonard Bernstein's musical recreation of Joan's medieval voices gives the play a new dimension."

In December conducts Copland's *Canticle of Freedom* for chorus and orchestra.

1956

On October 15 receives invitation to share music directorship of the New York Philharmonic with Dimitri Mitropoulos beginning in the 1957–58 season. This move comes after *New York Times* critic Howard Taubman attacks Mitropoulos for being "overmatched by the requirements of the post." Bernstein and Mitropoulos become increasingly estranged.

On December 1 *Candide*, a "comic operetta based on Voltaire's satire," opens at the Martin Beck Theater in New York, with music by Leonard Bernstein, lyrics by Richard Wilbur as well as John Latouche and Dorothy Parker, and book by Lillian Hellman. Directed by Tyrone Guthrie, the work runs for fewer than eighty performances. Walter Kerr of the *New York Herald-Tribune* writes: "Three of the most talented people our theater possesses—Lillian Hellman, Leonard Bernstein, and Tyrone Guthrie—have joined hands to transform Voltaire's *Candide* into a really spectacular disaster." *Time*, however, praises Bernstein's "verve and mocking lyricism" and "without being strictly eighteenth century . . . its gay pastiche of past styles and forms, a period quality."

1957

Awarded Emmy for Best Musical Contribution for Television by National Academy of Television Arts and Sciences for *Omnibus* broadcasts. Takes part in some three hundred televised programs in his lifetime and will receive twelve Emmy awards.

On September 26 *West Side Story* opens at the Winter Garden in New York. Preceded by enthusiastic receptions at out-of-town tryouts in Philadelphia and Washington, D.C., Bernstein's "tragic music-comedy" based on Shakespeare's *Romeo and Juliet* receives overwhelmingly favorable reviews from the New York critics—for Bernstein's score, for the lyrics by Stephen Sondheim, for the book by playwright Arthur Laurents, for the choreography and direct-

ing by Jerome Robbins, for the performances of Carol Lawrence, Larry Kert, and the electrifying Chita Rivera. Supreme Court Justice Felix Frankfurter reportedly tells Bernstein in the theater lobby that "the history of America is now changed."

In November Dimitri Mitropoulos announces his resignation, effective the end of the 1957–58 season, as music director of the New York Philharmonic, and Bernstein is engaged as the orchestra's new director, the youngest—and only American-born—conductor to assume that post.

1958

On January 2 leads his first New York Philharmonic concert since the announcement of his appointment as music director in November. He programs two of the same pieces that were played at his Philharmonic debut fourteen years before—Schumann's *Manfred* Overture and Strauss's *Don Quixote*—and performs as both pianist and conductor for the American premiere of Shostakovich's Concerto No. 2 for Piano.

With the New York Philharmonic, inaugurates an immensely successful new series for CBS-TV beginning in January, the *Young People's Concerts*. Includes such programs as "What Does Music Mean?" and "What Does Orchestration Mean?"

Goes on spring tour to South America with the Philharmonic: Bernstein and Mitropoulos lead thirty-nine concerts in twelve countries.

Opens his first full season as music director of the New York Philharmonic on October 2 with the new Thursday evening series of preview talks which provide a vehicle for Bernstein to speak about the music to the audience. Bernstein's first American season includes a general survey of American music that ranges from earlier New England composers like George Chadwick, Arthur Foote, and Henry Gilbert to later masters like Carl Ruggles and Charles Ives, whose Symphony No. 2 is on the opening program along with Beethoven's Symphony No. 7.

1959

In August and September takes the Philharmonic on a history-making tour of Western Europe, the Near East, and Russia. In Moscow he conducts the first performance of Stravinsky's *The Rite of Spring* in more than thirty years, as well as Ives's *The Unanswered Question* and his own *The Age of Anxiety*. He also meets his uncle Semyon, a Russian mining engineer, who is finally united after many years with his brother, Bernstein's father, Sam. Orchestra and conductor are both welcomed back to America as heroes.

In November the seven *Omnibus* scripts are collected and published by Simon & Schuster in Bernstein's first book, *The Joy of Music*.

Above:
Chita Rivera as Anita in *West Side Story*.
New York Public Library Performing Arts Research Center

Opposite:
Eva Marie Saint and Marlon Brando in *On the Waterfront*, released by Columbia Pictures, 1954. Bernstein's score was nominated for an Academy Award.
The Museum of Modern Art, New York, Film Stills Archive

149

1960

In January an ambitious Mahler Festival is inaugurated at the Philharmonic to celebrate the 100th anniversary of the composer's birth and the fiftieth anniversary of his debut as conductor of the orchestra. During the remainder of the season, performances of Mahler Symphonies Nos. 1, 5, 9, and the first movement of No. 10 are led by Mitropoulos while Bernstein follows with Symphonies Nos. 2 and 4 as well as the *Kindertotenlieder* and other songs with orchestra. The venerable Bruno Walter also appears, conducting *Das Lied von der Erde.*

On October 1, after a summer Philharmonic tour of the continental United States, Hawaii, Canada, and Berlin, Bernstein opens the 1960–61 season with the first of a concert series dedicated to "Schumann and the Romantic movement."

1961

On January 19 in Washington, D.C., at President John F. Kennedy's Inaugural Gala conducts his *Fanfare,* which has been specially composed for the occasion. Later in the year on November 24, Bernstein, along with a number of prominent musicians, including eighty-four-year-old Pablo Casals, is invited to the White House for a special party honoring Governor Muñoz-Marin of Puerto Rico.

On February 13 his friend Lukas Foss conducts the Philharmonic in the first performance of what will become Bernstein's most frequently performed concert work, the Symphonic Dances from *West Side Story.* The program also includes "Valentine Surprises," a special tribute to Bernstein from such friends as Carol Lawrence and Edie Adams, with Betty Comden and Adolph Green presiding over the ceremonies.

During the summer begins work on the third symphony, *Kaddish,* at Martha's Vineyard.

The new Philharmonic season is centered on the "Gallic approach" and includes appearances by Bernstein's longtime friend Jennie Tourel (in Berlioz's *Cléopatre*) as well as the influential French teacher of so many American composers, Nadia Boulanger, who conducts works of her sister, Lili.

1962

In January attends a small dinner party at the White House honoring Igor Stravinsky.

On February 5 and March 11 two innovative television features, "Leonard Bernstein and the New York Philharmonic in Japan" and "The Drama of Carmen," are presented on a Ford-sponsored series of programs produced by Robert Saudek and directed by William A. Graham for CBS. The Japanese program shows Bernstein at his most ebullient, introducing traditional Japanese music and dance as well as

accompanying Japanese singers in a rehearsal of *Trouble in Tahiti.* In the *Carmen* broadcast, Bernstein reintroduces the spoken dialogue of Bizet's original version (performed by Broadway actors Zohra Lampert and James Congdon) and compares it to the recitatives and arias (sung by Jane Rhodes and William Olvis) to show how the dramatic thrust of the initial version has been diluted by the addition, after the composer's death, of sung recitatives.

On February 28 birth of daughter Nina Maria Felicia.

On September 23, at the historic opening of Philharmonic Hall in the Lincoln Center for the Performing Arts, Bernstein conducts the world premiere of Copland's difficult *Connotations for Orchestra,* the Gloria from Beethoven's *Missa Solemnis,* and the rarely performed Part 1 of Mahler's Symphony No. 8 *(Symphony of a Thousand),* the "Veni, Creator Spiritus," whose immense orchestral and vocal forces—including two massed choirs—provide a true test for the new auditorium. After the exhausting performance he plants a controversial backstage kiss on a surprised Jackie Kennedy.

In the autumn publication of second book, *Leonard Bernstein's Young People's Concerts for Reading and Listening,* by Simon & Schuster.

1963

In August completes *Kaddish,* his Symphony No. 3 for Orchestra, Mixed Chorus, Boys' Choir, Speaker, and Solo Soprano. He is finishing the orchestration of the work on November 22 when he learns of President Kennedy's death.

On November 24, two days after the assassination, Bernstein conducts the New York Philharmonic in a performance of Mahler's *Resurrection* Symphony with soloists Jennie Tourel and Lucine Amara; it is televised live on CBS as *A JFK Memorial.*

On December 12 conducts the world premiere of *Kaddish* in Tel Aviv.

1964

In January the New York Philharmonic's "Avant-Garde Series" includes two movements of the extremely complex *Symphony* by Stefan Wolpe (conducted by Stefan Bauer-Mengelberg, a former Philharmonic assistant conductor) and new works by experimental European composers, including Xenakis *(Pithoprakta)* and Ligeti *(Atmospheres),* conducted by Bernstein himself.

On March 6 conducts first of ten performances (nine are in New York, one is in Boston) of Verdi's *Falstaff* in a lavish Franco Zeffirelli production at the Metropolitan Opera House. Falstaff is sung by Anselmo Colzani; Mistress Ford by Gabriella Tucci; Mistress Quickly by Regina Resnik; Fenton by Luigi Alva; Nannetta by Judith Raskin; Meg Page by Rosalind Elias; and Ford by Mario Sereni.

Left:
Robert Rounseville and
Barbara Cook, Candide and
Cunegonde in original
production of Bernstein's
Candide, 1956.
*Museum of the City of New
York, Theater Collection*

Opposite top:
With conductor Dmitri Mitropoulos, 1957, following
announcement of Bernstein's
appointment as music director of the *New York
Philharmonic*.
Bettmann Archive

Opposite center:
With New York Philhar-
monic at Carnegie Hall,
leading first televised Young
People's Concert, January
1958.
*New York Philharmonic
Archives*

Opposite bottom:
With Jerome Robbins, ca.
1957, the choreographer-
director of *West Side Story*.
New York Public Library

1965

Composes *Chichester Psalms* commissioned by Walter Hussey, dean of Chichester Cathedral, while on sabbatical from the Philharmonic. The work is premiered July 15 by the Philharmonic, Bernstein conducting.

In the fall inaugurates the Philharmonic season with the new series, "Symphonic Forms in the Twentieth Century." One of the highlights of the series is Bernstein's own performance of Mahler's Symphony No. 7 on December 2–6.

1966

On March 14 achieves a tremendous personal triumph with his performance of Verdi's *Falstaff* at the Vienna State Opera. Critic Rudolf Klein, in a review from Vienna for *The New York Times*, writes: "A comparable production of *Falstaff* has not been seen since the already legendary performances under Toscanini."

In November announces his intention to leave the New York Philharmonic at the end of the 1968–69 season, prompting a conciliatory article by his severest critic, Harold Schonberg, in *The New York Times*: "Bernstein: Wrong Time to Leave?"

Bernstein's autumn performances with the Philharmonic include an important revival of the *Airborne* Symphony by his friend Marc Blitzstein.

In November *The Infinite Variety of Music* is published by Simon & Schuster.

1967

In June conducts another performance in Vienna—this time of Mahler's *Resurrection* Symphony with the Vienna Philharmonic and the State Opera Chorus (soloists: Hilde Gueden and Christa Ludwig) in a special performance at the opera house.

Conducts Israel Philharmonic in concert on Mount Scopus, in Jerusalem, after the Six Day War.

In November Bernstein's New York Philharmonic recordings of Mahler's nine symphonies are released by Columbia Records in a sumptuous leather-bound set, receiving enthusiastic critical praise and becomes a popular success.

December 7 is the 125th anniversary of the first concert by the Philharmonic Society, and Bernstein leads the orchestra in a duplication of that December 7, 1842 performance, which includes arias by Mozart, Weber, Beethoven, and Rossini, as well as the first movement of Hummel's Piano Quintet in D minor, Opus 74, with Bernstein himself at the piano.

1968

On April 13 conducts first of five performances of Richard Strauss's *Der Rosenkavalier* at the Vienna State Opera. British critic Peter Heyworth describes the performance as having the "impact of a newly cleaned picture. Detail . . . lain buried under a patina of dirt and varnish (in this case a brown soup of string tone) has emerged with startling quality."

August 25, Bernstein's fiftieth birthday, is celebrated by a concert version of *Candide* in Philharmonic Hall.

In the fall Bernstein begins his final season as music director of the New York Philharmonic.

1969

On April 30 death of Bernstein's father, Sam. A week later, at Philharmonic Hall, Bernstein conducts *Jeremiah*, which he had dedicated to his father thirty years before.

On May 17 closes his eventful stewardship of the Philharmonic with a moving performance of Mahler's Symphony No. 3. After the performance he is presented with a gold and silver mezuzah by the musicians.

On May 25 returns to Vienna for a performance with the Vienna Philharmonic (and soloists Christa Ludwig and Walter Berry) of Beethoven's *Missa Solemnis* in honor of the 100th anniversary of the Vienna State Opera.

1970

On January 8 conducts first of five performances of *Cavalleria Rusticana* at the Metropolitan Opera House in New York, his second collaboration with designer-director Franco Zeffirelli. Cast includes Franco Corelli as Turiddu, Grace Bumbry as Santuzza, Nedda Casei as Lola, Frank Guarrera as Alfio, and Carlotta Ordassy as Lucia. Chooses not to conduct the traditional companion work, *I Pagliacci*, which is led by Fausto Cleva.

In April, to celebrate the 200th anniversary of Beethoven's birth, conducts the Ninth Symphony with the Vienna Philharmonic and Boston Symphony orchestras in their respective cities within six days of each other. Writes to Austrian critic Fritz Endler of *Die Neue Presse*, Vienna, of Beethoven's "charm" (reprinted in *Findings*, 1982): "To play Beethoven's music is to give oneself over completely to the child-spirit . . . in that grim, awkward, violent man, to go all the way with him as he cries out *Brüder! Töchter! Freude! Millionen! Gott!* [Brothers! Daughters! Joy! Masses! God!] We must believe it in order to play it."

In the spring films the Verdi *Requiem* in London, and, in June, Beethoven's *Fidelio* in the Theater an der Wien (Vienna)—the site of the original production—to commemorate the 200th anniversary of Beethoven's birth. He is also presented with Austria's Gold Medal, one of the country's highest civilian decorations.

In August and September tours Japan and the southern United States with the New York Philharmonic.

Above:
Bernstein, right, and pianist Seymour Lipkin, at the Tchaikovsky Conservatory, Moscow, following a performance by the New York Philharmonic, 1959.
Photograph by Don Hunstein, Sony Music

Opposite:
Bernstein in rehearsal for the John F. Kennedy Inaugural Gala, Washington, D.C., January 19, 1961.
Photograph by Dennis Stock, Magnum

153

1971

On September 8 premiere of *Mass*, subtitled "A Theater Piece for Singers, Players, and Dancers," which is composed for the opening of the John F. Kennedy Center for the Performing Arts in Washington, D.C. Dedicated to the slain president, in whose honor the composer uses the traditional Catholic Mass as a framework, it engages modern dance, Hasidic rhythms, and rock-band instrumentation in its portrayal of the spiritual crisis in the contemporary world. Principal singer is Alan Titus and the principal dancer is Judith Jamison; choreographer is Alvin Ailey, and conductor, Maurice Peress.

On December 15 conducts his 1,000th performance with the New York Philharmonic, a number not reached by any other conductor.

On December 24 American television viewers have the opportunity to see Bernstein's distillation of his Viennese musical experiences performing Beethoven—both as conductor and pianist—in the film *Beethoven's Birthday: A Celebration in Vienna.* Produced independently, the film was finally purchased and shown by CBS after Bernstein's personal appeal to William Paley.

1972

On March 28 Two Meditations from *Mass* for Violoncello and Piano premieres in New York at a memorial concert for Abraham Friedman held at the Institute of International Education. Stephen Kates and the composer are the performers. Meditation III from *Mass*, for orchestra, performed in Jerusalem on May 21 by the Israel Philharmonic Orchestra, withdrawn from the Bernstein catalog.

On September 19 opens the Metropolitan Opera season by conducting the first of six performances of Bizet's *Carmen.* The production was conceived and was to have been directed by Goeran Gentele, Sir Rudolf Bing's successor as general manager, who was killed in an automobile accident just a month earlier; Bodo Igesz directs, following Gentele's notes. The cast includes Marilyn Horne as Carmen; James McCracken as José; Adriana Maliponte as Micaëla; and Tom Krause as Escamillo, the toreador. Shortly thereafter, the production is recorded by Deutsche Grammophon with the same principals.

1973

On January 19, with the National Symphony Orchestra, leads the Concert for Peace at the National Cathedral in Washington, D.C.

On October 9 delivers first of six lectures as the Charles Eliot Norton Professor of Poetry at Harvard. Bernstein titles his series of lectures "The Unanswered Question" after the visionary Charles Ives piece; in them, using the psycholinguistic models provided by M.I.T. linguist Noam

Chomsky, he explores the phonology, syntax, and semantics of music.

On December 9 delivers eulogy at funeral of Jennie Tourel.

On December 20 a new production of *Candide*, produced by Harold Prince, opens in Brooklyn's Chelsea Theater. The orchestra, reduced to thirteen members, plays a score newly arranged by Hershy Kay. Among other important changes are the new book by Hugh Wheeler, additional lyrics by Stephen Sondheim, and Prince's circuslike, theatre-in-the-round production. On March 5, 1974, the production moves to the Broadway Theater, where it runs for 740 performances.

1974

On May 16 *Dybbuk*, a new ballet with music by Bernstein and choreography by Jerome Robbins, opens the New York City Ballet's spring season. Based on the Yiddish play by S. Ansky, the work dramatizes the possession of a young woman by a demon. Bernstein derives his music from the cabalistic numerology that forms such an integral part of medieval Jewish mysticism.

1975

On April 3 conducts the first U.S. performance of *Dybbuk Suite No. 1* with the New York Philharmonic and with Paul Sperry, tenor, and Bruce Fifer, bass-baritone, at Avery Fisher Hall in New York. The American premiere of Suite No. 2 occurs on April 17. (The first performance of both *Dybbuk* suites took place in New Zealand in 1974 under the title *Dybbuk Variations.*)

1976

In February, Harvard University Press publishes his fourth book, *The Unanswered Question*, based on the Norton lectures.

On May 4 the musical *1600 Pennsylvania Avenue* premieres in New York City after extensive revision during the out-of-town tryouts in Philadelphia and Washington, D.C. The show closes soon after, its critical reception almost unanimously poor.

On October 28 the separation of Bernstein from his wife, Felicia, is made public.

1977

On January 19 conducts "To My Dear and Loving Husband," from *Songfest*, at the Inaugural Concert for President Jimmy Carter at Kennedy Center in Washington, D.C.

In March and April the Israel Philharmonic presents a two-week festival of Bernstein's music in celebration of the thirtieth anniversary of his first performance with the orchestra.

Left top:
Seated at the piano, conducts musicians from the Vienna Philharmonic in a chamber recital at the Schoenbrunn Palace, Vienna, April 14, 1966.
Bettmann Archive

Left bottom:
Receives audience's applause and an appreciative smile from Willi Boskovsky, left, concertmaster of the Vienna Philharmonic, after a performance in the Musikverein, Vienna, 1969.
Photograph by Elfriede Hanak

Opposite top:
SOLD OUT! New York Philharmonic on tour, Teatro alla Scala, Milan, September 1968.
New York Philharmonic Archives

Opposite center:
Recording Mozart piano concerto with the Vienna Philharmonic, in Vienna, March 6, 1966.
Photograph by Elfriede Hanak

Opposite bottom:
Rehearsing Mahler with New York Philharmonic, Lincoln Center, New York, May 1967.
Photograph by Don Hunstein, Sony Music

155

On October 11 Mstislav Rostropovich conducts *Slava!*, a piece written especially for him by Bernstein; only three and a half minutes in length, it makes use of a tune salvaged from *1600 Pennsylvania Avenue*. *Songfest* and Three Meditations from *Mass*, conducted by Bernstein, also premiere.

1978

On January 29 conducts *Fidelio* at the Vienna State Opera House in a live telecast to eighteen countries. It is broadcast in America on February 21, 1979.

On June 16 death of Felicia Montealegre Bernstein in East Hampton, Long Island.

On August 28 the Leonard Bernstein Sixtieth Birthday Celebration Concert at Wolf Trap, Virginia, with the National Symphony Orchestra conducted by Mstislav Rostropovich, is telecast internationally.

On November 22 conducts the European premiere of *Songfest* with the Bavarian Radio Symphony Orchestra in Munich.

1979

On September 16 visits Nadia Boulanger in a Fontainebleau hospital on her birthday. Bernstein asks her if she still hears music. When she answers yes, he asks her which of her favorite works she "plays in her memory." She replies: "A music that has no beginning or end." From Léonie Rosenstiel, *Nadia Boulanger: A Life in Music*, 1982.

1980

On September 25 premiere of Divertimento for Orchestra, commissioned by the Boston Symphony Orchestra on the occasion of its centenary year. The fourteen-minute work is conducted by Seiji Ozawa at Symphony Hall, Boston.

On October 11 premiere of *A Musical Toast*, dedicated to André Kostelanetz and played by the New York Philharmonic, Zubin Mehta conducting.

On November 14, at an eightieth-birthday celebration for Aaron Copland, conducts his *Lincoln Portrait*, narrated by the composer, with the National Symphony Orchestra in Washington, D.C.

On December 7 receives Kennedy Center Honor for Lifetime of Contributions through the Performing Arts. President and Mrs. Carter are in attendance at the ceremony in the John F. Kennedy Center for the Performing Arts, Washington, D.C. Also honored are soprano Leontyne Price, choreographer Agnes de Mille, and the actors Lynn Fontanne and James Cagney.

1981

On May 27 conducts premiere of *Halil* (Hebrew for "flute"), his Nocturne for Solo Flute, String Orchestra, and Percus-

sion, with the Israel Philharmonic in Tel Aviv. Jean-Pierre Rampal is soloist.

On June 12, in honor of Pope John Paul II, conducts *Kaddish*, *Halil*, and Three Meditations from *Mass* with the Orchestra dell'Accademia di Santa Cecilia at the Vatican, in Rome.

On December 4 inducted into the fifty-member American Academy of Arts and Letters; he occupies the chair formerly held by Samuel Barber, who died earlier in the year.

1982

In January and February, as Fellow-in-Residence at Indiana University in Bloomington, begins work on a new opera, *A Quiet Place*, with librettist Stephen Wadsworth; together they direct workshops on the new opera.

In July and August serves as artistic director of the Los Angeles Philharmonic Institute in California, where he gives master classes in conducting.

On October 13 the third, opera house version, of *Candide* opens at the New York City Opera, John Mauceri conducting.

1983

On June 17 premiere of the first version of *A Quiet Place* at the Houston Grand Opera with John DeMain conducting. The cast includes Sheri Greenawald as Dede, Tim Nolan as Junior, Peter Kazaras as François, Chester Ludgin as Sam. Choreographer is Grethe Holby, and Peter Mark Schifter is director. The opera is commissioned jointly by the Houston Grand Opera, Teatro alla Scala of Milan, and the John F. Kennedy Center for the Performing Arts in Washington, D.C. It is a sequel to *Trouble in Tahiti*, which is performed on this occasion with Edward Crafts as Young Sam, and Diane Kesling as Dinah.

On August 25 his hometown, Lawrence, Massachusetts, celebrates Leonard Bernstein Day to acknowledge the cause of nuclear disarmament. Festivities include a parade, a concert, and the dedication of an outdoor theater named in his honor at Heritage State Park.

On December 31 first New Year's Eve appearance at the Cathedral of St. John the Divine, New York, where he speaks out for nuclear disarmament and world peace. It becomes an annual event for the rest of his life.

1984

On June 19 premiere of revised version of his opera *A Quiet Place* at Teatro alla Scala, Milan. It is conducted by John Mauceri, who is in large measure responsible for the work's revision; *Trouble in Tahiti* is now incorporated into the second act as a flashback.

On July 19 performance of *A Quiet Place* at the Kennedy

Above:
Crowds arriving for a Bernstein Charles Eliot Norton Lecture, Harvard Square Theater, Cambridge, Massachusetts, 1973.

Opposite:
The Bernstein family, Jamie, Leonard, Felicia, Alexander, and Nina, in their apartment in the Dakota, New York, 1976.
Photograph by Henry Grossman

Top:
With beard and ever-present cigarette in Vienna, 1976.
Photograph by Elfriede Hanak

Bottom:
With Stephen Wadsworth, ca. 1986, the librettist of *A Quiet Place*, their opera of 1983.
Photograph by Henry Grossman

Opposite:
Surveying a rehearsal of *1600 Pennsylvania Avenue*, 1976, at the Mark Hellinger Theater, New York.
Photograph by Henry Grossman

Center, Washington, D.C., Mauceri conducting.

Beginning September 4, over a four-day period, conducts recording of *West Side Story* with soprano Kiri Te Kanawa as Maria, tenor José Carreras as Tony, and mezzo Tatiana Troyanos as Anita. Bernstein's operatic version of his 1957 Broadway musical is one of the most successful recordings ever issued by its publisher, Deutsche Grammophon. The sessions are filmed for television.

On November 21 honored by the Boston Latin School on the anniversary of its founding 350 years before. Given an award for "outstanding achievement in his field."

On December 2 Bernstein's daughter Jamie is married to David Evan Thomas.

On December 31 makes second New Year's Eve appearance at St. John the Divine. His friend Ned Rorem writes: "With Shirley [Gabis Perle] this bleak afternoon to [the cathedral] where a crowd of thousands assembled to hear Bernstein conduct 'A Concert for Peace.' He also spoke from the pulpit with the brevity of genius, the word *AIDS* ringing bravely into the midst. Later Lenny received in the only area that resembles a dressing room—a little chapel behind the altar—and offered Scotch to everyone."—*The Nantucket Diary*, 1987.

1985
In July and August conducts European Community Youth Orchestra in Journey for Peace. They travel to three European cities—Athens, Budapest, and Vienna—and to Hiroshima; there, on August 6, the fortieth anniversary of the Japanese city's devastation by an atom bomb blast, they play two concerts in which his *Kaddish* (from the prayer in Jewish ritual chanted at graveside) is the central work. The final concert in the series is on August 11, at the Vienna State Opera, where they play to an overflowing house; a giant television monitor is set up outside so that the throngs in the square below can take part in the event. Bernstein shares conducting duties with Eiji Oue.

On September 26 opening of *Bernstein: The Television Work* at the Museum of Broadcasting, New York, where programs ranging from his early *Omnibus* series to later international broadcasts are shown. An accompanying catalog lists all programs he has made to date, many in the museum's permanent collection.

1986
On April 10 conducts his opera *A Quiet Place* at the Vienna State Opera.

On April 29 opening of two-week festival devoted to Bernstein's music at the Barbican Center, London, sponsored by the London Symphony Orchestra. Bernstein conducts *Chichester Psalms*; Serenade for Solo Violin, Harp, Percussion, and String Orchestra; and *The Age of Anxiety* in a concert

attended by Queen Elizabeth and the Duke of Edinburgh.

On August 4 conducts New York Philharmonic in a concert on the Great Lawn of Central Park, New York, attended by two hundred thousand people. It is his first performance there since 1976.

On September 12 leads premiere of *Jubilee Games* for orchestra, with the Israel Philharmonic at Avery Fisher Hall in New York. It is dedicated to the Israel Philharmonic on its fiftieth anniversary.

On December 15, celebrating the reopening of Carnegie Hall, conducts the New York Philharmonic in a performance of *Opening Prayer*, his newly composed benediction for the New York landmark.

1987
On March 4 his daughter Jamie gives birth to his first grandchild, Francisca Ann Maria.

In April and May conducts a workshop (along with Jerome Robbins, John Guare, and Stephen Sondheim) on musical adaptation of a Brecht play, *The Race to Urga*, at the Mitzi Newhouse Theater at Lincoln Center. The work remains uncompleted.

In August receives the Edward MacDowell Gold Medal at the MacDowell Colony in Peterborough, New Hampshire.

On November 8, at Music for Life, the AIDS Benefit Concert at Carnegie Hall, conducts the symphony orchestra especially assembled for the occasion in the Overture to *Candide* and the Adagietto from Mahler's Symphony No. 5.

1988
On May 9 premiere of *Arias and Barcarolles* at benefit for Young Concert Artists at the Equitable Center Auditorium, New York. Singers Joyce Castle, Louise Edeiken, John Brandstetter, and Mordechai Kaston perform with Bernstein and Michael Tilson Thomas as pianists.

On May 11 sings the first performance of a new song, "My Twelve-Tone Melody," written in honor of Irving Berlin's 100th birthday, at Carnegie Hall.

On May 21 John Mauceri conducts the first performance of the expanded version of *Candide* in Glasgow.

On July 26 conducts first of three concerts in Moscow with the Schleswig–Holstein Music Festival Orchestra.

Seventieth birthday celebration, August 25–28, at Tanglewood.

New Mahler recordings: the Second Symphony with the New York Philharmonic; the Fourth Symphony with the Amsterdam Concertgebouw; the Fifth Symphony with the Vienna Philharmonic.

1989
Birth of his second grandchild, Evan Thomas.

On December 25 conducts Beethoven's Ninth Symphony in East Berlin and West Berlin; 220,000 East Berliners enter West Berlin and 257,000 West Berliners enter East Berlin.

1990
On March 9 performs for the last time with the Vienna Philharmonic at Carnegie Hall.

In July artistic director, with Michael Tilson Thomas, of the newly created Pacific Music Festival, Sapporo, Japan.

On August 21, at Tanglewood, conducts "Four Sea Interludes" from *Peter Grimes* and Beethoven's Symphony No. 7, his final performance.

On October 14 death of Leonard Bernstein in New York. He is buried in Greenwood Cemetery, Brooklyn, New York.

On November 14 the music world's memorial to Bernstein in Carnegie Hall.

On December 13 Broadway's memorial to Bernstein at the Majestic Theater.

New Year's Eve Memorial Concert on December 31 at the Cathedral of St. John the Divine; students from Tanglewood, the Schleswig-Holstein Festival Orchestra, and the Japanese Pacific Music Festival Orchestra participate.

With the family in Connecticut, 1989. From left, Bernstein, his son Alexander, daughter Nina, granddaughter Francisca Ann Maria, daughter Jamie, and, in front, son-in-law David Evan Thomas, who holds his son Evan, Bernstein's second grandchild.
Photograph by Henry Grossman

near her
death